Walls
OF MY
Heart

Dr. Bruce Thompson

and Barbara Thompson

CROWN MINISTRIES
INTERNATIONAL
P.O. Box 49 Euclid, MN 56722

Other Materials by Bruce Thompson
The Divine Plumbline Video Series
The Divine Plumbline Audio Album
The Divine Plumbline Study Guide

Scripture Quotations:
THE AMPLIFIED BIBLE. Old Testament copyright 1965, 1987 by the
Zondervan corporation. The Amplified New Testament copyright 1958,
1987 by The Lockman Foundation. Used by permission.
HOLY BIBLE: NEW INTERNATIONAL VERSION. Copyright 1973,
1978, 1984 by International Bible Society. Used by permission of Zonder-
van Publishers.
REVISED STANDARD VERSION. Second Edition copyright 1972 by
Division of Christian Education of the National Council of Churches of
Christ in the United States of America. Used by permission.
GOOD NEWS BIBLE. Old Testament copyright 1976, New Testament
copyright 1966, 1971, 1976 by American Bible Society. Used by permission.

Published by:
Crown Ministries International
P.O. Box 49, Euclid, Minnesota, 56722

Printed in the United States of America

Library of Congress Catalog Card Number: 88-92665
ISBN 0-935779-13-2

A WORD ABOUT
THE AUTHOR'S WORK

Tens of thousands of people around the world have benefited from the writings and teachings of Dr. Bruce Thompson. His series of lectures that deal with the wounds and hurts that we all receive and how they affect our personalities, have been liberating, healing, and helpful to leaders, Christian workers and laymen. His new book, *Walls Of My Heart*, makes it possible for many more people to benefit from this wonderful teaching.

Every Christian leader should be exposed to the understanding that God has given Bruce, as it will help us to understand those we work with. **Every Christian** who has a longing to serve the Lord will want to read this book. It will help you understand yourself, your disappointments, your insecurities, your ambitions and how you can more effectively serve God.

Local churches and Bible schools will want to use this book as a study for classes and Christian growth courses. Its practical benefits are immeasurable as well as being very Biblical teaching. I very highly commend it to you.

Floyd McClung, Jr.
Executive Director
International Operations
Youth With A Mission

PREFACE

During the early 1970's, my wife Barbara and I lived on a remote mission outpost in Northern Ghana. Besides working in a leprosarium and a small general hospital, we began developing a mobile medical work, living among the Africans in the villages for several days each week. We became well acquainted with the rural African lifestyle, and medicine began to take on a new perspective. We found ourselves not only treating the ailments of the people, but also considering how to prevent some of their suffering in view of their lifestyle. Before long we had embarked on an exciting total health care experience where we not only attended to their physical needs but also to their emotional and spiritual needs as well.

Upon returning to New Zealand in 1973, we continued this venture by developing a center for healing of the whole person in conjunction with a team of clergy. Many people were touched and blessed. Later we were led to go to Kailua-Kona, Hawaii, and develop a counseling ministry for Youth With A Mission (YWAM), an international and interdenominational missionary organization. Since 1976, the ministry has grown into the College of Counseling and Health Care, one of the seven colleges in YWAM's University of the Nations, now being developed in many locations world-wide.

The concepts recorded in this book and taught in a college course, have arisen out of my life experiences in Africa, New Zealand and Hawaii. Patients, counselees and students have been my teachers, and my overall instructor has been the Holy Spirit. My key resource text: the Holy Scriptures, which are God-breathed and profitable in all matters pertaining to life.

Proverbs 4:23 states that the most vital issues of life arise out of the heart. There is a sense in which we all realize this, and as a result build up defensive walls around it. These walls of false protection often evolve into the walls of our personal prison, locking in our true personality.

Our study finishes with a look at what the Bible reveals as the whole, mature personality God planned for each of us to be. I pray you will experience this change, as you give yourself to its truth and reach out to your full maturity in Him.

Should you need help in working through any of the issues discussed, I recommend that you get in touch with a pastoral or professional Christian counselor in your area.

To all my patients and friends who have taught me so much: Be assured of the confidentiality in all case histories presented here. Names have been changed and situations altered so no one can be identified or embarrassed. Perhaps you will think you see yourself, but remember, many are going through the same trials and experiences.

It is to you, my patients and students, whose search for life and truth have unearthed this volume, that this book is dedicated

"... That [we might arrive] at really mature manhood - the completeness of personality which is nothing less than the standard height of Christ's own perfection - the measure of the stature of the fullness of the Christ, and the completeness found in Him."

Ephesians 4:13, Amplified Bible

Bruce R.T. Thompson.
1988

ACKNOWLEDGEMENTS

First, I want to thank my two sons, Michael and Lionel for sharing us with this time consuming project. Secondly, I express my deep appreciation to my dear wife Barbara, who has logged many hundreds of hours at the computer writing, rewriting, and editing this text. She has also headed up an able team of editors and critics with the valuable and close assistance of Meredith Puff. Others on this team include: Larry Carlson, Jane Crane, Mel Hanna Ph.D., Shawna Morgan, Ron Noll Ph.D., Janice Rogers, Iris Schreuder, Luella Tate, and Diane Wicker.

Gary Johnson, Don Traller and Alan Robbins have given valuable input through their computer expertise. Steve Steckler of Crown Ministries International has made a valuable contribution in the text arrangement, as well as editing and logging hundreds of hours at the keybord. Dale Buehring, director of Crown Ministries International and his wife Evie have been a constant encouragement and have not let us give up along the way. Dale's expertise in production and marketing has been a real blessing to us as well.

A special thanks to Jean Darnell for her prophetic ministry into our lives, and also to Brian Pollard and Terry Dugan for the cover design.

Our thanks to the staff of the College of Counseling and Heath Care, who have not only prayed, but also have gone many extra miles to enable us to complete this text.

Finally, we are grateful to Loren and Darlene Cunningham, along with the Pacific and Asia Christian University council for their much valued encouragement and input into our lives, out of which this work has emerged.

TABLE OF CONTENTS

My anguish, My anguish! I writhe in pain!
Oh, THE WALLS OF MY HEART
My heart is beating wildly;
I cannot keep silent;
For I hear the sound of the trumpet,
The sound of war.

Jeremiah 4:19
Revised Standard Version

CHAPTER ONE

IN OVER MY HEAD

It was a sultry, hot April afternoon. Beads of perspiration formed on my brow as I hurried across the parking lot. Above, brooding storm clouds scudded across the blue bowl of the sky forecasting another tropical storm.

"At least the rain will lower the humidity for a while," I mused, noting how the usual brilliance of the Hawaiian day was subdued and still, waiting expectantly it seemed, for the storm to be released. The fragrance of the plumeria permeated the air filling my nostrils with tantalizing aroma. Pushing open the door, I stepped into the welcoming coolness of the counseling office and began to look over the schedule for the rest of the day. My first appointment was to be with a newcomer to the clinic, a Larry Coombs.

Sharply at two he arrived, tall and lean with dark hair neatly combed in place. Greeting him, I noticed that his long slender fingers fidgeted with his clothes and he had the distracting habit of chewing on his moustache. Though the room was dimly lit, I was surprised he made no attempt to remove his sunglasses.

"How do I break through this reserve?" I thought. What could I say that would cause this man to relax a little and let down some of his defenses?

A DIFFICULT SITUATION

For several weeks I had been seeing Larry's wife, a Christian on the verge of a breakdown. Larry's lifestyle of alcoholism and drugs was not only eating up their resources, but also destroying their relationship. Together she and I were praying for Larry. Only two days ago, she had phoned excitedly to say that he would see me.

Now, as I looked at him slumped in one of the orange canvas chairs, his head turned away, I wondered how I could help. I began to ask some gently probing questions.

"Larry, did your father spend time with you? Did he discipline you?"

I leaned forward to catch his muffled, almost incoherent words. Several minutes passed, and then, as though unable to sit still any longer, he got up and paced back and forth. A torrent of words burst out.

"Father! Ugh! He never cared for me. He'd lash out at me and knock me down. I never knew when he would fly off the handle." He nervously tugged on his moustache. "I don't ever remember him saying that he loved me!"

As he moved restlessly back and forth in the small confining room, he continued, "I do remember the time I - ah, stole something. Just some little thing. Dad was so angry that he marched me down to the police station and left me there for a week. He said he wanted to teach me a lesson.

That did it for me! I vowed that I would never trust him again!"

What little I could see of Larry's face still hiding behind his sunglasses had taken on the appearance of marble - hard and cold.

"Larry, how old were you when it happened?"

"Twelve or thirteen."

I noticed he clenched his fists as he continued venomously. "He was so unfair, so unjust! He always thought about himself. As soon as I could, I ran away from home."

Larry sank back into the chair, once again guarded, and my attempts to get him to talk about himself again were futile. He obviously was not going to trust me with any more information. My secretary tapped on the door indicating that my next appointment had arrived.

"Our time is up for today, Larry."

I tried to conceal my frustration. A fleeting look of relief passed across his face and he rose moving for the door handle.

"Larry, I'd like to see you again."

"Alright," he mumbled and dashed out the door.

Later, alone in the office, I looked at the notes I had jotted down while Larry was speaking. He had been so guarded in what he had revealed that I felt perplexed. How could I help him? I had circled words like insecure, fearful, anxious, and humiliation. Something about Larry's pent-up anxiety took me back to a painful experience I had when I was just eight years old.

POTENT MEMORIES

The scene was again so vivid. I felt like it had happened yesterday. I saw my fourth grade teacher, tall and surly with short-cropped, graying hair. She was not among the best of my friends. One morning she asked me to find out the time in another classroom. The school clock was big and round with large black hands that were easy to see, so the request seemed simple. But as I hurried down the wide, wooden corridors, it suddenly hit me - I couldn't tell time!

Staring at the big school clock, I fought a rising surge of fear. How could I admit the truth to the whole class? Minutes ticked by as I stood there wrestling with myself. Finally I had an idea - perhaps I could guess the correct time! As I entered the room, all eyes focused on me as they waited to hear my answer.

"Um, ahh, six o'clock," I mumbled.

For an instant the teacher looked at me with raised eyebrows. Suddenly she began to smile, and the snickers from my schoolmates burst into open laughter. I could feel my face reddening, and my lips began to tremor. Wiping my sweaty hands on my shirt, I dashed to my desk and tried to hide behind my books.

To make things worse, the teacher began to use my point of vulnerability on other occasions to lighten the mood of the class. The more it happened, the more fearful and withdrawn I became. Finally any classroom participation caused my stomach to go into a thousand knots. Whenever I made a mistake she would rap my knuckles with a ruler, until I came to dread her. I couldn't even look her in the face.

A COMMON BOND

Remembering my own pain now gave me new insight into Larry's struggle as I saw some parallels between our stories. We both had struggled with a harsh authority figure, looking and hoping for love and understanding, but instead finding injustice and wounding. It took me years to work through those resulting emotions that had left me quivering like jello on a plate. Feeling overwhelmed, I put my notes away and began to prepare for my next client.

A week later Larry was back again. Slaty low-hanging clouds hid any shafts of sunlight from penetrating the dark room, but Larry hid behind his sunglasses. At least he seemed less fearful and agitated. Relaxing in a canvas chair next to mine, he began to talk freely. I still detected his inner restlessness as I listened, but at least he was not pacing back and forth like a caged lion.

Larry confided he had become a hippie as a young teenager, throwing himself into a life of immorality and mainline drug abuse. Soon he became involved in crime to support his habit, going from one broken relationship to another. Now married, with a wife and child, he was trying to trust people, but often he would explode in rage whenever hurt or let down.

I leaned forward, asking, "How do you feel about what is happening to you?"

He moved restlessly on the sagging chair, nervously drumming his fingers on the wooden armrest.

"Lonely. I'm really getting depressed. Scared too. Scared about what I might do to my wife and kid when I get into a rage."

I nodded as he continued on, and we were both more relaxed by the end of the session. As I ended with prayer, then reached over and squeezed his arm, there was the glimmer of a smile on his lips as he promised to return.

Once alone in the office, I sat back in my chair and pondered what I had heard. I faced a greater challenge than any before. There were so many broken pieces to Larry's life. Could they ever be put together again? He was like a Humpty Dumpty and I faced the challenge of being all the king's men.

"Lord I need you!" I cried, "I need you to unlock the door of this life before it's closed forever." I didn't know that this would be the start of a great revelation and a new phase in my ministry.

FINDING THE ANSWERS

By the time Larry returned for his third counseling session I felt I had something new to give him. I had sought the Lord since our last meeting and sensed there were some keys to his problems that God was going to reveal.

"Hi! How ya doin'?" Larry said entering the room. Flopping down in a chair, he leaned back while a small sigh escaped his lips.

"Fine, thanks Larry," I replied, fighting hard to hide my surge of relief at his relaxed manner. "Well, what kind of week have you had?"

"Better. I've been giving a lot of thought to what we've been talking about," he answered. "Yeah, I even talked over some things with my wife."

As we went on to talk about relationships, I asked if he had ever experienced a loving relationship before. He shook his head.

"No, not until I'd met my wife." He went on to describe how she had stood by him and refused to abandon him no matter what. Instead of criticizing and condemning him, as others had before, he felt for the first time that somebody really cared for him.

"I find it hard to accept," he said. "I've always felt in the way and that no one cared what happened to me." As we continued to talk about his wife's love and what it meant to him, slowly, hesitantly he reached up and removed his sunglasses. For the first time in three weeks, I saw his eyes: dark brown, almost black. They were moist with tears and filled with brooding emptiness.

A breakthrough! I wanted to jump and shout for joy, but instead, I quietly breathed a prayer of thanks. He went on talking about his broken relationships with his parents and some difficulties with his wife, while I went to my office blackboard.

Pondering the dynamic of parental influence in Larry's life, I picked up some chalk and began to draw some lines, not quite sure what I was going to do. Suddenly my thoughts began to crystallize. I drew a line at a 45 degree angle, representing the rejections in Larry's life. As we began to review those wounding experiences together, I saw that the level of Larry's rebellion, his involvement with drugs and crime, had really come out of his experiencing rejection. From the top of that line, I drew another angled line to form the large inverted "V" with the two lines meeting at the top. This second line I used to represent his rebellion. (See diagram on page 8.)

As we talked together about the diagram, I began to see the link between significant authority figures in Larry's life. Larry had received rejection from his father and his time in prison had wounded his spirit. He had made a vow never to trust his dad and I was seeing the results being worked out in his life. Now he couldn't trust anymore. By rebelling and moving into a life style of immorality, crime and addiction, he was actually expressing his rejection.

Larry leaned forward in his chair. His eyes, riveted on the board, mirrored back a glimmer of hope.

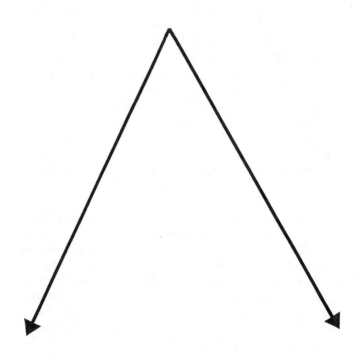

REJECTION   **REBELLION**

"Hey! You're making sense!" he said with a slight grin tugging at the corners of his mouth.

Now flicking through the pages of my Bible, I searched for confirming scriptures to support what I had been saying. My mind raced ahead, finally putting together some of the pieces that had been missing from the puzzle of Larry's life, as well as my own. It was clear that I had stumbled onto a significant truth concerning the influence of authority figures in our lives. When Larry later left the office, my secretary commented on his smile and bright eyes. I was elated!

THE HEALING PROCESS

In the ensuing weeks I saw Larry on a regular basis. Little by little, I doggedly presented God's standard for living found in the Bible. Larry began to change. His eyes became clearer and a new peace pervaded his being, replacing his former restlessness. I took him through steps of repentance helping him see his responsibility for the choices he had made - choices that had pulled him to the depths of despair.

yes "Repentance," I explained, "is taking responsibility for your own life and making a deliberate choice to turn from self-destructive practices, to good, wholesome, godly ones."

I then counseled him to read the scriptures and pray daily in order to maintain what God had extended to him through His mercy. It was a different Larry who saw me for the last time. It was a Larry who had experienced a touch of God in his spirit and had exchanged torment for peace.

A NEW CHALLENGE

His life and the lives of others who came seeking help challenged me. How could I help Larry and those like him? What tools could I use? I began to earnestly search the scriptures for answers and further revelation. Then one day I discovered an exciting truth that related to what I had drawn on the blackboard that day. Amos chapter seven speaks of Israel being like a wall out of line with God's plumbline. Looking it up in both a concordance and a dictionary, I found that a plumbline is an instrument used by builders to ascertain the precise vertical direction of a wall.

As I pursued this thought, I saw that the line I had drawn in representing rejection in Larry's life, was a false plumbline, as was the line representing his rebellion. Both lines were out of line with God's original plan - His Divine Plumbline - that lay somewhere between the two false, human plumblines.

This was the place that Larry had been searching for, but never seemed to find. Instead, he was always lined up with one of the false plumblines of rejection or rebellion that had been dropped into his life through his parenting and other authority figures. When Larry came into my office, his life was tottering over him like a wall out of line, threatening to tumble down. At the same time, I had been on the verge of an important revelation that had been building up in my life over many years, unbeknown to me. Larry's life had become like a switch that turned on lights in the darkened rooms of my past.

The sea glinted and sparkled, reflecting back a myriad of colors. It was a lovely day, warm with clear blue skies. I sat on a jagged piece of lava rock dangling my feet in a tide pool and soaking up the hot Hawaiian sun.

My mind was busy roaming the corridors of my life, while my family built sand castles on the small stretch of beach. It was just yesterday that I told Larry that I would not need to see him again. For him, it was not the end, but the beginning, and I realized for me it was also the beginning of my search for greater revelation. Larry had stimulated me to look back into my own life in a fresh way, and as I sat relaxing in the sun, I allowed my thoughts and memories to take me back to the past.

WHAT SHALL I DO WITH MY LIFE, LORD?

I became a Christian at the age of thirteen through the "Boy's Brigade" ministry. A year later, at a Baptist Bible camp in rural Cambridge, New Zealand, God began to speak to me about being a missionary. I had struggled through what seemed to be endless years of study to pass my university entrance exams before I faced the question - what would I do with my life? The thought of going on to university was joyless, so it came as a surprise when on of my friends asked if I had considered medicine.

"Medicine!" I laughed. "That's too much! You've got to be kidding! I'm sick of school!"

But over the next weeks, his comment shimmered in the back of my mind, firmly planted. Words of scripture began to leap out of the page, highlighted. Comments from other people confirmed my inner convictions. Then I discovered that the three new subjects I had randomly chosen to qualify for the entrance exams - biology, chemistry and physics - were exactly what I'd need at medical school! God was clearly confirming my call into medicine, quite against my better judgment. Instead of going right into the mission field with no training, I would become a medical missionary.

Starting pre-medical studies in university I conscientiously studied from dawn until deep into the night. The competition was challenging and only a small percentage of students who applied for medical school would be accepted. It came as no surprise that I failed to qualify at the end of the year. Accepting this as the norm, I determined all the more to succeed.

Once again I gave myself to hours of endless study to take the exam again. Once it was over, I impatiently and anxiously waited for the results. What happened next is etched vividly in my mind never to be erased. Full of anticipation and excitement I tore through the town on my 150cc Italian motor scooter to join a chattering group of students standing before the notice board. Quickly my eyes scanned the alphabetical list of names for my test results. P - Q - R - S - Ttt - Thompson? Thompson! Where was my name? Horrified, I realized it wasn't there. That could mean only one thing. I had failed again!

THE AWESOME PAIN OF REJECTION

Stunned and trying hard to hold back the tears, I realized that though I had done well, I still hadn't made it into the accepted upper echelon. With leaden feet and a heavy heart I retraced my steps. A storm raged within me.

"I'm a failure! I always knew I was. I'm dumb! Hopeless!" Thoughts of self-condemnation and of self-pity flooded my mind. I would just quit this silly pursuit and go right to the mission field! All the negatives programmed into me over the years were there, reinforcing my sense of failure and worthlessness. The whole system seemed so wrong. I'd studied so hard. Much harder than many of those colleagues whose names were on the list. In fact, I later learned that I had passed my exams. But for now I agonized, "Why couldn't they accept me?"

Throwing myself down beside a small stream on campus, I began to release my pent up feelings by crying out to God.

"Where are you God? Don't You care?" Thumping the ground to ease my frustration, I began to blame Him. "I'm only here because You called me and now You have let me down."

For weeks I wrestled back and forth questioning God and His character. Like Job of old, I demanded an explanation. If there was none forthcoming then I would feel justified in dropping out of the program and moving toward the mission field. That must have been it! I felt like I had God in a corner where He could find no escape. So I decided it must be right to drop out and escape years of long and arduous study.

I was beginning to feel comfortable in my planned course of action, when God came out of His corner one night with overwhelming conviction! As I prayed, God showed me that I would be of little use to Him on the mission field with a heart that had not learned the most basic of His messages: "To obey is better than sacrifice."

COMMITTED TO GOD'S WILL

Slowly I began to see God was more interested in my spiritual qualifications than He was in my degree. He was telling me to obey. With a heavy heart, I dragged myself back to the discipline of medical studies.

For the next six years I sweated over my text books determined to succeed no matter what. It was a day of victory and triumph when, at the age of 28, I received my Doctorate in Medicine. After years of arduous study, I had at long last reached my goal. Finally I could be a medical missionary.

For one year I travelled with the inter-denominational ministry, Youth With A Mission (Y.W.A.M.), evangelizing in various nations of the world, ending up in Ghana, West Africa. Here the door was wide open to work with Worldwide Evangelization Crusade, commonly called W.E.C. As with YWAM, the goal of WEC is to reach the unevangelized parts of the world. Along with my wife Barbara, we developed a mobile medical ministry, daily facing the challenge of imparting the gospel to primitive tribes whose main object in life was finding enough food and water to live. In our struggles to communicate, we discovered a way into their hearts through medicine and saw several churches emerge and grow where previously there had been none.

Four years later we returned to New Zealand for what we thought would be a year's rest. Instead, I found myself working in a busy general practice, seeing one patient after another. When stumped with a patient's medical problem, as I often was, I would pray under my breath, asking Jesus for help in making the right diagnosis and prescribing the correct treatment. But my deepest frustration came in recognizing that without a change in many of my patient's life styles, they would be back sooner or later with a reoccurrence of their diseases.

One day I had an opportunity to share my frustration with the elders of the fellowship we attended. They not only offered the use of the church facility, but also several of the staff to work with my wife and me in what became a counseling and health care center. Before long, the center's heavy work load necessitated my resignation from private practice to be full time in the new medical ministry. Those days had reached their height of fulfillment when God interrupted what we thought was our life's ministry - He called us to Hawaii! Our reticent elders confirmed it and 18 months after our work had begun, we found ourselves on an Air New Zealand jet headed for Honolulu.

NEW HORIZONS

"Welcome to Kona!" Our smiling air hostess pushed various levers to open the exit door amidst lilting Polynesian music filling the cabin.

"Kona, Hawaii!" I murmured to myself. "This can't be Kona. It looks like we've landed on the moon!" As I peered out of the small plane window, a vast expanse of black lava rock met my puzzled eyes. Heat waves shimmered and shook across the runway. In the distance a mountain loomed, while to our right, the warm Pacific crashed against the jagged shoreline. My wife Barbara struggled with her emotions as well as our three-year-old son, Michael, a ball of energy who challenged us at every turn. Picking up Lionel, our chubby 15-month-old, I started out the exit.

No one seeing us deplane that January day in 1976 would have ever guessed we would ever spend more than a decade in Hawaii - especially not us! Our church fellowship in Palmerston North, New Zealand, had released us for three years so I could help establish a medical program for Youth With A Mission.

The challenge was to develop a mobile medical

unit that could be easily transferred onto a ship or taken anywhere in the world. I was soon to find out that God had a different plan for my life. After a few futile attempts to commence such a work, I received a letter from the licensing board saying that in order for me to be licensed as a medical doctor in the State of Hawaii, I would have to do a three year internship in a state licensed hospital, plus take my final exams again!

I felt bewildered and confused. Here I was with a wife and two children, miles away from home, confident of God's leading, only to have the door slammed shut in my face! What made it worse was that Barbara was convinced that I had moved ahead of God. She wasted no time telling me. Her response was one of exasperation.

"Good!" she exclaimed. "Now we can pack our bags and go home."

For her, Hawaii was no paradise and Youth With A Mission, struggling for existence in those pioneering days, only added fuel to her convictions that we had made a mistake in leaving our fulfilling and satisfying ministry in New Zealand.

PERSEVERING

I wavered back and forth in my double-mindedness. Had I heard the voice of God or was it presumption? Were we to go back home, or did God have something else in mind? As the struggle intensified, I reviewed both my guidance and the circumstances. But amidst all the voices that clamored for attention, I could not shake the inner conviction that quietly encouraged me. At last, I wrestled through to a decision to stay on and ride out the storms, hoping that some helpful landmarks would appear to guide the way.

Those landmarks proved to be a long time

coming, and in the interim it *seemed* that we lost everything overboard. We had no ministry or medical practice, in contrast to our full involvement in New Zealand. In addition to these difficulties, our son, Michael, had a close shave with death. While playing with some of his friends, he crashed through some rotten railing and fell 20 feet onto a concrete path below. We rushed him to the hospital, fearing the worst, finding he had a hairline fracture of the skull and a large hematoma obscuring his right eye. But many of our new friends in Hawaii and those back home prayed for Michael. To our relief, he made a rapid recovery with no after effects.

As we set about doing odd jobs for the growing YWAM ministry in Kona, some landmarks did come into view. We began to see some of God's purposes in calling us to Hawaii.

One day while talking to Loren and Darlene Cunningham, the International Director of YWAM and his wife, we shared about our thriving counseling ministry back in New Zealand. When we told Loren that God had clearly shown us that medicine was to complement the primary ministry of counseling, he suggested we pray about it together. One after the other, we each received strong impressions that God was pointing to a new ministry within YWAM. Both Barbara and Darlene were directed to Isaiah 54:2-3, telling us to enlarge the place of our ministry, "lengthening our cords and strengthening our pegs." God seemed to be saying that the ministry would expand all of our expectations.

After visiting several counseling clinics across the United States and finding two people to help us, we started our first counseling clinic in Kona in January, 1977. It was here we met Larry, and others like him, and God began to release key truths to unlocking the hidden doors in their lives. Soon God led us to begin counseling seminars to train others and multiply the message worldwide. After several years, the seminars grew and developed into degree granting programs at Youth With A Mission's Pacific and Asia Christian University in Kona, Hawaii. Later they were spread to other nations in the form of extension schools of the University.

In this book I will share the biblical approach to wholeness and healing that I have learned over my years of study and ministry. Embark with me on this voyage of discovery of your true self in the light of the most reliable reference on life ... the *Divine Plumbline.*

CHAPTER TWO

SOMETHING'S OUT OF LINE

In the 8th century B.C., during the reign of Uzziah, king of Judah, the nation of Israel was being borne along on a rising tide of prosperity and peace. But along with this affluence came a rapid decline in morals, undermining society. A seamy smog of social injustice obscured Israel's view and it lost its divinely given direction.

Into this challenging arena God called Amos,[1] a shepherd and dresser of fig trees, to represent His cause. Amos' mission was to denounce the social and religious corruption and warn of God's impending judgment. Even his name, Amos, is related to a Hebrew verb meaning "to bear a load."[2] With Moses, God chose a rod to demonstrate His truth and values, but with Amos He chose a plumbline.

---

1. Amos 7:7-8
2. New Scofield Reference Bible. p.932.

A   PLUMBLINE

FIGURE 1

GOD'S MEASURING STANDARD

A plumbline in its simplest form is a small inverted cone of lead, attached by a cord to a cylindrical piece of wood of the same diameter. It is used by builders to ascertain the precise vertical direction for the construction of a wall. The weighted end always points toward the center of the earth, as it responds to an otherwise invisible force called gravity. (See Figure 1) Construction workers have found this simple but profound instrument of inestimable value. They realize that if their building is to be stable and stand, its studs and walls must line up with the plumbline. If not, the building could topple down.

Beneath Israel's affluence was moral decay. God depicts the nation as a wall that is out of line and about to topple down. To demonstrate the extent of that instability He drops the plumbline of His law alongside His people. He shows that any day the nation could fall and be scattered by its enemies as blocks of a wall. God has never ceased to extend the plumbline of His word alongside the lives of those He has called to be His people. He continues to do this with us, the people of this century, so we might know the truth and find the way to a stable, secure life.

THE BASIC QUESTION

We live in an age where many people no longer know or think about the plumbline of God's word. Yet this age is still greatly concerned with the question, "What is life and how should we live it?" The interest in this question is shown by the number of students who overflow psychology classes in

FIGURE 2

our universities and the growing tide of those who experiment in existentialism, new consciousness, drug trips, occultism, and other forms of altered reality. This basic question can be broken into four parts. The first is the fundamental question of ONTOLOGY: "WHO AM I?" In order to bring focus and definition to our answer, let's look at several characterizations of different personalities.

THE PASSIVE RESPONSE

First we see someone encased in "personality armor" as in Figure 2. As we view this person, what impressions come to mind? The following is a list of actual responses people have given while viewing Figure 2.

defensive	*vulnerable*
fearful	*passive*
blind	*deaf and dumb*
lonely	*depressed*
helpless	*hopeless*

The person encased in this armor is in an identity crisis, evading the "Who am I?" question. Previous attempts to deal with it have probably failed, so rather than face this question and the trauma it brings, the man hides behind his armor retreating from any threat to his identity.

THE AGGRESSIVE RESPONSE

Another personality who is wrestling with the same question is represented by the woman with the bow and arrow in Figure 3. In reviewing this profile, consider some of the qualities that may come to mind:

FIGURE 3

aggressive	*critical*
negative	*defensive*
resentful	*insecure*
lonely	*fearful*

Holding her bow and arrow, this woman demonstrates another approach to handling an identity crisis. Instead of the *passive* defensive mode, she adopts the more *aggressive* stance. Individuals approaching her are warned to either keep their distance or be wounded. The fact that the arrow is not drawn up in the bow indicates she does not really want to be aggressive, but will be, if necessary.

If we put these two together, we can see in some ways they could relate compatibly. The woman could shoot her arrows whenever she wanted, and at least he would know someone was around to ease his loneliness. Their communication system would be the ping of arrows hitting armor, without either party being hurt! All too often, this illustration sadly reflects the level to which many marriages and relationships deteriorate.

WHERE IDENTITY BEGINS

These two profiles are examples of individuals who have not succeeded in coming to know who they are. How do you try to answer this important question? In order to begin to resolve our own personal ontology and answer the "Who am I?" question, we need to go back to our own origin. The biblical thesis of origin states: "In the beginning GOD ..."[3] The Bible further unfolds the revelation of origin when Moses asks God to iden-

---

3. Genesis 1:1

ASKING THE FUNDAMENTAL QUESTIONS OF LIFE

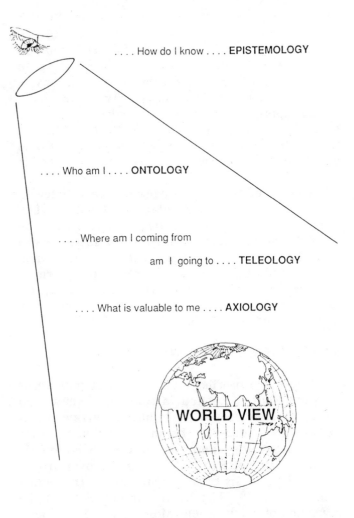

.... How do I know .... **EPISTEMOLOGY**

.... Who am I .... **ONTOLOGY**

.... Where am I coming from

am I going to .... **TELEOLOGY**

.... What is valuable to me .... **AXIOLOGY**

WORLD VIEW

FIGURE 4

tify Himself for the sake of the nation of Israel.[4]
God responds with the following: "I AM WHO I
AM" and "I WILL BE WHAT I WILL BE."

A further elaboration on identity is made in
the New Testament by JESUS, the Son of God. In
relating about Himself and His role among us, He
says:

> *"I am the Way, the Truth and the
> Life, no one comes unto the Father
> except by Me."*[5]

Let's examine what is being said in these two
passages. First, God is stating that all identity begins in Him. If we are to understand who we are,
then we must begin by coming to understand who
He is. He is the beginning of us all and our total
beings cry out to be related back to Him.[6]

Second, Jesus is describing Himself as the Way
to knowing God. He is God's Ambassador and is
therefore in a position to introduce us to His Father. Solving life's basic question of *"WHO AM
I?"* begins here.

THE COMPONENTS OF IDENTITY

To adequately answer the questions of "What is
life and how do we live it," we need to consider
three sub-questions as illustrated in Figure 4. The
first two are:

1. Where are we coming from?

---

4. Exodus 3:13-14, Amplified Bible
5. John 14:6
6. Psalm 42:1-2

2. Where are we going to?

These two questions relate to our history and destiny, coming under the term TELEOLOGY. Teleology speaks of the innate desire in all of us to have some direction or purpose in life. If we aim at nothing, we usually hit it! The Bible puts it this way: "Without a vision the people perish."[7] The welfare mind-set within society today has largely arisen from a lack of proper roles and life goals in people who have not adequately answered these two questions.

3. What has value to me?

This third question comes under the term, AXIOLOGY, meaning the important study of values. Every person has what is called a "value set," composed of everything in which we invest our lives, efforts, time and finances. We believe them to be worthwhile, so we value them enough to invest in them. Often there is a gap between the "head or intellectual" value set and the "heart or personality" value set. The former is expressed by what we say, while the latter is expressed by what we do. From the heart, life's vital attitudes and understandings issue forth.

HOW DO WE KNOW?

Fundamental to these three questions, is the question, "How do we know?" What lens do we look at our world through? We want to know how we can determine whether our knowledge is true or

---

7. Proverbs 29:18

not - and this is the question of EPISTEMOLOGY. But as Christians, we believe God has revealed truth to us. Jesus emphasizes that He is the Truth, as already mentioned, in John 14:6. The answers to all the questions of life and how to live are to be sought in God's revelation of Himself in His word and in His Son, Jesus. This is God's plumbline.

DISCOVERING YOUR WORLD VIEW

In coming to understand some of the answers to the question of existence, we begin to discover our own WORLD VIEW. Each of us has a world view, which in simple terms is a statement of what we believe and why we believe it. A more comprehensive statement would include an account of the origin, nature, and destiny of man and the cosmos, along with comment on man's role and purpose in the cosmos.

Much diversity exists in man's response to these fundamental questions of life, even in formal philosophy. It all depends on the epistemological lens through which he views the world. The following are short summaries of some of the world views espoused by philosophy as it has developed down through the centuries. Examples of each of the world views mentioned below can easily be found in the world today.

MONOTHEISM: One God and Father of us all.

POLYTHEISM: Many gods with delegated areas of authority and power.

ATHEISM: No gods at all. They are

only a figment of the imagination of man himself.

ATHEISTIC HUMANISM: If there is a god at all, it has to be man himself. Man is god.

ATHEISTIC RATIONALISM: Man acting out his godhood by extolling his own reason as the only means of arriving at truth.

ATHEISTIC EXISTENTIALISM: A non-rationalistic jump into the realms beyond the mind to grasp the meaning of individual existence. This is an indirect acknowledgement from a rational perspective that man fails at being God.

OCCULTISM: In man's leap into the unseen, non-sensory world to discover his identity, man finds himself with another god who calls himself "the god of this world,"[8] or Satan. Of course he is so cunning many of his subjects do not even believe in him, and yet serve him.

All these world views describe man's search for answers as he moves away from "I AM," except the

---

8. John 12:31

first one - MONOTHEISM. In POLYTHEISM, man puts divinity into the created entities affecting his life, e.g. the sun, the trees, the wind. In ATHEISM man says to the I AM: "You are not!" In his next breath, man has had to say, "The only I AM for sure is ME," meaning man. With God out of the picture, we see man trying to be god in the world views of atheistic HUMANISM and atheistic RATIONALISM.

In EXISTENTIALISM, we see man move away from a rationalism, cut off from the central issues of life, to look for another way to validate his existence. As he exhausts all his inner resources for self-authentication, it is only a short step to reach out into the world of spirits to discover another force or influence. Without realizing it, this brings man into the power of "the prince of this world"[9] as he slips and slides rapidly into OC-CULTISM.

This whole cycle is designed to seduce man out of the gentle hands of a loving God and into the bondage of being a slave of Satan. There is a God shaped void in every human heart and man must fill it somehow or live in a spiritual vacuum.

GOD'S PURPOSE

In the brief survey above, it becomes apparent why so many people find themselves in an identity crisis while struggling to answer life's fundamental questions. Once we brush aside, "I AM," we lose touch with the source of truth about "WHO I AM." This is exactly what happened to Israel in the time of the prophet Amos. When they chose not to have God as the source of their lives, God called Amos to the scene to bring them back to the place where

---

9. 2 Corinthians 4:4

FIGURE 5

JEHOVAH was their GOD and His truth was their plumbline.

The nation Israel had wandered so far away from God that He described them as a tottering wall out of line which could tumble down at any time.[10] (See Figure 5.)

This image of a tottering wall and a plumbline held at perfect vertical powerfully illustrates the difference between a world view where God is central compared to one where He is not. Some of these differences are:

> absolutes versus relativity
> law versus opinion
> order versus chaos
> freedom versus slavery

Without God as our reference point, we are lost to life and all it could mean.

KEEPING TRUE PERSPECTIVE

A number of years ago while I was ministering in Poland, I learned a valuable lesson about maintaining a true reference point. Across the way from my accommodations was a forest, and being a lover of outdoors, it didn't take much to entice me to take a prayer walk. Setting out in the early summer freshness, I sighed with contentment as I saw the rays of the sun filtering through the canopy of deciduous trees.

Communing with God at each step, I was caught up in the loveliness of my surroundings and the One who made them. Of course I paid little

---

10. Amos 7:7-8

attention to such mundane things as where I had been and where I was going.

It took a few more twists and turns down the crisscrossing network of footpaths before it hit me. I was lost! Feeling rather foolish, but confident of my vague recollections, I began to randomly select paths which seemed familiar, only to become more confused as I delved deeper into the now unfamiliar forest. A feeling of absolute hopelessness began to engulf me, as well as the sinking sense of being utterly lost.

Now I couldn't spot one single familiar reference point to get me out of my predicament. Every tree and every path looked the same! So I had no absolute indicators to follow. All ideas of where to turn were relative to my unknown position. I was totally, completely lost!

Standing there in the midst of this fearful predicament, I realized I was finally at the end of my own resources. I looked up through the towering trees to the patches of overcast sky above, and a thought simply came to me. "He can see where I am - why not ask Him?" I had left the best source of information to the last!

Following God's promptings, I began to walk, first down one path and on to the next. In what became an enjoyable game with my heavenly Father, I found myself guided to the edge of the forest, where I was then able to find the way back to my lodgings. All I could do was praise the Lord for His faithfulness as I briskly walked along.

This experience has given me a vivid and unforgettable link to the people who live out their lives with a sense of being lost and without direction. It has caused me to ponder the absurdity of multitudes of people who do not ask God for the Way until the last years of their lives, or who die in the "Forest of Lostness."

THE WALLS OF MY HEART

While God likens us to a wall, it's not the wall that's the challenge. The challenge lies in changing the heart around which the wall was constructed! God brings His plumbline alongside the heart of a man as well as a nation. In the book of Proverbs[11] we are admonished to keep our hearts with all diligence, as out of it are the issues of life. Our tendency has been rather to guard or keep our mind and intellect, as if life's issues were really centered in our education. But from Proverbs, we clearly see they are not.

THE "HEART" DEFINED

The Bible uses the term *heart* in several ways. In the Hebrew language, two of the words used for heart are "leb" and "lebab." In reviewing the context for the use of these words in the Bible, we can find 204 occurrences where these words are translated with an emphasis on the "mind." In 195 places, these words are translated with an emphasis on the "will," while 166 times they are used in the framework of the "emotions." But, the most frequent use of these terms, in 257 occurrences, focuses on the whole of the inner person, or the "personality."[12]

The Greek word translated "heart" is "kardia," which continues in common usage in modern medicine, e.g. cardiac disease. From our brief study, we can see that the "personality" is equal to the whole of the inner person, meaning the soul plus the

---

11. Proverbs 4:23
12. New Bible Dictionary, J.D. Douglas, Editor, (Grand Rapids:Eerdmans,1962) p. 1375.

spirit. It is the changeable aspects of the inner man or personality that God brings His plumbline alongside, holding us accountable for what we develop in our lives.

CONCLUSION

Sociologists have highlighted the ongoing "Nature verses Nurture" controversy. The nature side of this argument states that people are largely determined by inheritance and cannot change. The nurture side emphasizes that we have learned to behave as we do and that what we have learned can be modified. Most people today recognize we not only can change, but in most cases that we desperately need to change in order to LIVE. A change of mind may not necessarily result in a changed life, but a changed heart definitely will!

Just as a building inspector uses a plumbline to ensure that a structure is safe to be in, so God uses the *Divine Plumbline* to evaluate the building of our lives. The measure to which they are out of line with His standards reflects the degree of insecurity, instability and vulnerability we feel in the stresses and strains of life. As we begin to move our lives back toward His plumbline, we begin the exciting adventure of discovering "I AM-ness!"

CHAPTER THREE

ASSAILED BY STORMS

"He's a hypocrite! He tells lie after lie," Anne exploded.

Patiently I listened, as this silver-haired grandmother, married for more than 30 years, began to release her pent-up emotions. Some 20 years previously her husband had been unfaithful. He had truly repented and sought to put things right, but over the years, like a slow growing cancer, doubts and fears had grown in this woman's heart. Now she was sure. He had lapsed back into adultery. Why, he had hugs for every woman that crossed his path.

"He holds hands with different ones far longer than necessary. And I have even found him fantasizing with some of my undergarments."

She told how, when she confronted him, he had reacted with hurt and anger, saying it was all in her mind. But she knew - just knew, he was having an affair and that he kept lying to her.

I prayed with her and promised to explore her marital crisis further. After speaking with her husband and two of the ladies he was accused of hav-

ing relationships with, the truth began to unfold.
Ever since her husband had been unfaithful to her,
Anne had struggled to trust him. Now that their
children were grown and away from home she had
lots of time on her hands. With time to think, she
became paranoid and critical of the least interaction
her husband had with the opposite sex.

It became apparent as I talked to her again that
she had been deeply deceived and her fears of
betrayal had clouded over her perception of truth.
This degree of self-deception was robbing both her
and her marriage of realizing their full potential
through discovering their identity or their "I AM-
ness." Her "self talk," or the words she dwelt on
inside her own mind, had become a false prophet
leading her deeper into deception and despair.
Only by recognizing this and adjusting her life to
God's divine plumbline could she be free.

Likewise, in our search for significance, it is
imperative we be aware of the false plumblines or
paths we may follow along the way. The ease with
which we can be seduced or sidetracked from the
main path is amazing. What is often called common sense may more truthfully be called common
deception, as our own reasoning often leads us
astray.

FALSE PROPHETS

False prophets, both those inside and outside
our inner beings, are a constant threat to God's
people. In Ezekiel[1], God expresses His wrath
against those who proudly proclaim messages and
visions supposedly from Him, but in fact, are not.
As a result of these lies, the Israelites built their

---

1. Ezekiel 13:15-16

lives with flimsy, unstable walls, covering them with whitewash. While the false prophets applaud them for their efforts, God warns impending storms will sweep away the whitewash and bring their fragile, false walls crashing to the ground.

Hidden in this imagery is a further elaboration of the theme introduced to us by Amos[2] regarding walls. Illustrated in Figure 6, we see someone standing behind the fragile wall of fear he erected to protect himself. This person has apparently experienced inner trauma and no longer wants to be vulnerable. However, as he lives behind his wall, he finds himself unable to enjoy deep, warm friendships, and often is lonely. He may even experience periods of deepening depression, as well as harbor deep-seated feelings of resentment, bitterness and even hatred toward those who have offended him.

How did this person learn to build these teetering walls? Who showed him the need for them, and how to use bricks of negative qualities to construct them? Over and over I've seen it to be the following false prophets which have rashly and unwisely uttered words which never passed from the lips of God. Both subtly and directly, through modeling and influence, they have exhorted their audience to build up walls of fear and mistrust, even in the name of the Almighty. Who are these false prophets and what platforms do they use to so deceive us?

PARENTS

The first false prophecy in our lives may come to us through parents. Even the best, all too sadly,

---

2. Amos 7:7-8

FIGURE 6

misrepresent God and His truth by failing to talk and walk in His ways. Because of the present-day crisis in failing to rear children within a Biblical framework, the need for re-parenting is often discussed.

For example, Julie grew up hearing her mother tell her, "You are a wicked, bad little girl! God hates you!" It's no wonder why she grew up hating herself, deeply depressed for years. She believed this awful lie about God and herself, and her mother proved to be a false prophet in shaping her life.

In another case, a father attempted to spur his son on in his studies by regularly lashing out at him. "Bonehead!" "Dummy!" and "Hopeless case!" were Judah's daily fare. By the time I first saw him, Judah was in his thirties. He described through sobs how he lived out his dad's labels, dropping out of high school and abusing drugs and alcohol in order to silence the condemning voices echoing within his mind. Negative words eroded his self-confidence over the years, when actually, with his above average IQ, he could have easily completed a college degree.

When it comes to predictions about children's abilities, looks, or future, children will receive these words literally, especially coming from their parents, the most important people in their lives. Many parents don't realize they are as God to their young children, who take their words as final and true. Such unkind, false statements can cripple a child's emotional development, holding him back from a normal life.

TEACHERS

If teachers so choose, they may inflict deep-seated wounding in the spirit of a child by false accusations, or unjust management. Once, while speaking at a large high school assembly on morality and its importance in life, I noticed discomfort among some of the staff. I later learned several of the teachers, including the principal, had been promising good grades and references in return for sexual favors from some of the students. Needless to say, I was not invited back to that school. The teachers were manipulating students into immorality, showing them this was the way to progress and succeed in life.

The complications of pregnancy and VD were not of course discussed by these manipulative masters. Fortunately, the teachers were later brought to justice when one of the pregnant girls informed her parents of the truth. Other girls followed suit and several teachers were forced to resign.

PEERS

We are in an age today where legalism is being greatly eroded by liberalism in an attempt to discover freedom. There is no arena that so greatly exemplifies this as that of sexuality. Teens especially are under much peer pressure to become sexually active before marriage. The peer false prophets advocate sex as a legitimate way for an unmarried couple to end an evening together, and resent professing love without sexual intimacy. Terms like "recreational" and "casual" sex are commonplace and socially acceptable.

The National Academy of Sciences[3] reported the results of this peer prophetic ministry, by stating that 64% of teenage boys and 44% of teenage girls in the U.S. are sexually active by the time they are 18 years old.

But these false prophets fail to give the whole message relating to immorality. They don't discuss taking responsibility for what could be theirs nine months later. Neither do they proclaim the possibility of a lifetime of pain and discomfort through a herpes infection, or the potential of sterility and infertility through a chalamydia infection, not to mention the increasing possibility of death from the AIDS virus.

The **new cases** of these sexually transmitted diseases (S.T.Ds.) in the United States were reported as follows:[4]

	1986	1987	1988
Herpes	250-500,000	250-500,000	250-500,000
Chalamydia	4,500,000	4,500,000	4,500,000
AIDS	13,097	20,620	(to Oct.10) 25,021

The teen abusers of sex are either ignorant of, or choose to ignore these fun-killing facts! "If it feels good do it," they prophesy. The "in" message is, "Different strokes for different folks! So get it together! Don't be a nerd!" With this kind of pressure they ensnare a large portion of our teenage populace. We are desperately in need of true teen prophets who will stand for real life and its abundance.

---

3. National Academy of Science, December 10, 1986
4. Center For Disease Control, Atlanta, Georgia estimates on the herpes and chalamydia infections. "AIDS Weekly Surveilance Report" (CDC) for AIDS figures, October 15, 1988.

GOVERNMENT

Many governments also take the role of false prophets, proclaiming falsehoods to their people, and even exerting force to ensure they are heeded. From capitalism to communism, democracy to autocracy, governments legislate and administrate laws that are detrimental to their people. They often work to incriminate the one who will not compromise the truth.

When Israel decided against a theocracy[5] in Samuel's day, they opened the door for false prophets to lead the people into all kinds of problems and injustices, of which Samuel warned them.

> *"A King will take your sons and make them serve with his chariots and horses. Some he will assign to be commanders of thousands and commanders of fifties, and others to plow his ground and reap his harvest, and still others to make weapons of war and equipment for his chariots. He will take your daughters to be perfumers and cooks and bakers. He will take the best of your fields and vineyards and olive groves and give them to his attendants ... he will take the best of your cattle and donkeys for his own use ... and you yourselves will become his slaves."*

But the people refused to listen and insisted on having a king, like all the other nations. God told Samuel it wasn't him they rejected, but they were rejecting God as their king. And, just as Samuel warned, such false prophets entered in to cause

---

5. 1 Samuel 8:11-14, 16-17; NIV

warned, such false prophets entered in to cause them misery, as will happen to us if we choose any other than God's true prophets to guide our lives.

MEDIA

The media is perhaps the most sinister and malignant of all the false prophets, setting up its altar in almost every home in the developed world. The whole family sits at its feet for daily worship, as it exalts lifestyles of lust, violence and crime in subtle but salient ways. Dr. William Dietz[6] calculates that the average American elementary school child watches 12,000 violent acts a year on TV, and spends anywhere from 11 to 26 hours a week in front of the tube. Other surveys reveal that prime time shows average 13 violent scenes an hour, and cartoons even more.

Sadly, the newspapers' top stories are often a re-enactment of the violence on these TV and movie features:

A young man upset with life and wrestling with deep wounds of rejection, emerged into the busy main street of a bustling city. Dressed up in a cowboy outfit complete with wide brimmed hat, leather boots and spurs, he wore a six-shooter snugly over each hip. Stepping out in front of the traffic, he gave a fancy flick of the wrist, drew both guns and began to fire indiscriminately at the cars.

Pandemonium broke out as panicking people raced around trying to find cover. Some ran like rabbits, darting in and out between the cars in an attempt to get out of range. A satisfied smirk

---

6. William Deitz, former chairman of the American Academy of Pediatrics' Task Force on Children and Television.

in the power of pumping lead from his snarling six-shooters.

This is not an excerpt from a movie - it actually happened in a major city several years ago. The police, after surrounding the cowboy, persuaded him to throw down his weapons and took him into custody. He was later sentenced to life imprisonment.

Media men don't know how greatly they affect society with their sordid tales, turning their fantasies into real life tragedies.

Messages also run off the pen of prophets, proclaiming the godhood of man and a myriad of other lies never found on the lips of God.

Many video stores and clubs now evade local censorial laws, giving license to whosoever wills to be passively programmed by the media's false prophets.

THE CHURCH AND ITS LEADERS

One thing church history seems to have taught us is how little we have learned from it. We seem to continue repeating its events from one generation to the next, with leaders rising to fame only to fall in shame, again and again. The church has certainly had its share of false prophets as well.

The Bible records many examples of false prophets who misdirected and misled the Israelites. Ezekiel[7] talks about the foolish prophets who follow their own spirit seeing falsehood and lying divination, saying, "The Lord says; but the Lord has not sent them." The church has become so diverse in its expression of truth that an outsider

---

7. Ezekiel 13:3,6; Amplified Bible

may easily decide not to bother associating with it.

Some "Christians" have assembled on a mountain to wait for Jesus to rapture them on a certain date, only to be disappointed. Other "Christians" have followed leaders into social suicide in total deception. Still others have believed in faith for healing, yet died from a disease that could have been treated by modern medicine.

Now in more recent years TV evangelists who have openly spoken out against sin and all kinds of immorality, have been exposed as being involved in it themselves.

The church at large has given the world such a mixed bag of messages it's no wonder many no longer come to hear even true prophets proclaim God's truth.

THE HEART

In the book of Jeremiah[8] we are introduced to one of the most powerful transmitters of false prophecy - one often overlooked. In fact, many are led astray by its "still small voice." Though the *heart* is often trusted as truthful and reliable, the Bible tells us it is deceitful. The heart can be dishonest and misleading, without our even being aware of it, and some even say, "If you don't feel it in your heart, don't believe it." This misconception gives the heart a dangerous place of authority, and so deceives many.

All of these false prophets, and others, may exhort and direct us in the wall-building process, telling us these walls are the only means of survival against life's threats. "Without a wall," some say, "there's no life at all!" But we need to distinguish

---

8. Jeremiah 17:9-10

"there's no life at all!" But we need to distinguish between the deceptive voice of these false prophets, and those truly sent by God, or the walls we build will come crashing down in storms of adversity.

STORMS

The passage in Ezekiel[9] goes on to describe wind, hail and rain storms that hurl themselves against the wall to bring it down. Let's consider some of the storms that may assail the walls within our lives.

HEALTH	*DEATH*
DIVORCE	*ECONOMICS*
DRUGS	*ALCOHOL*
DELINQUENCY	*VOCATION*

As we put the pictures of this passage in Ezekiel together, we will understand its underlying message. Like so many of us, the little man illustrated in Figure 6 has built up his own defense system, symbolized by the wall. Of course in his blindness, he fails to see both his vulnerability and his inability to participate in deep, loving relationships.

What if he hears the gospel and becomes a Christian? Does this mean everything changes and his wall is dissipated? Not necessarily. It does mean the light goes on, and for the first time he begins to see himself behind his wall.

His first natural response is to cry out to God for help, but as he persists in prayer, a storm brews. The more he prays the more intense the

---

9. Ezekiel 13:9-16

storm becomes. Suddenly a brick topples down alongside him! More and more bricks fall, until finally his whole wall is shattered. His first reaction is alarm, then fear, followed by total devastation.

As the dust begins to clear, we see one of two things. Either it's a clenched, angry fist shaken in the face of God, followed by accusations of injustice, unfaithfulness, unfairness, and lack of love *or*, we see a bowed head with tear-streaked cheeks from a broken and contrite heart, which the Lord says He will never despise. The former man with the clenched fist rises to rebuild thicker and stronger walls, while the broken man leaves bricks behind and enters into a new lifestyle, uncluttered by his brick-bound past.

Storms are always significant to the one who seeks life. *What did you glean in truth and life from your last storm? Or will you need to go through the storm again before its message affects your life toward a desirable change?*

THE ULTIMATE DECEIVER

Of all the false prophets, none are so cunning and deceptive as Lucifer himself. In the scriptures he is often described as a serpent. Amos 5:19 illustrates Lucifer's strategy in the walls of our personality in his attempt to rob us of our inheritance in life.

As we let our imagination develop the story of Amos 5:19, we might envision the following:

One dew-drenched, pre-dawn morning, a farmer made his way to his fields, walking briskly along the narrow bush path against the chill in the

FIGURE 7

filled with thoughts about the day's work before him. Passing by a grove of cedar trees, he suddenly became aware that he was not alone. Stopping, he peered around, all senses on the alert. As he strained for any sound to reveal who or what lurked in the shadows, silence enveloped him like a blanket. Nothing. With an audible sigh he again started to walk, when suddenly, a lean, shaggy lion bounded toward him from amongst the trees. Spinning around with adrenalin pumping into his body, the farmer almost flew back down the path. Aware that he had somehow outrun the lion, he stopped to catch his breath and recover from his fright.

Not daring to use the same path again, the farmer then chose another way to go to his farm - an old river bed winding its way amongst the rocks. The sun was already climbing the pale blue bowl of sky, causing dawn shadows to flee. The man hurried, picking his way among the rocks and boulders. Rounding a bend, he then to his horror saw a huge bear barring the way. Growling threateningly, the bear flailed his front paws. Overcome with fright, the farmer managed to mobilize his shock-frozen feet and raced back down the river bed. Now he relinquished all thought of work, at least for that day!

Arriving home exhausted and drained, the farmer leaned back against the wall of his house to regain his composure. Just as he relaxed and let down his guard, out from the wall emerged a snake. With a sudden strike, the snake's fangs pierced his arm!

The farmer was able to escape both the outer enemies of the lion and the bear but succumbed to

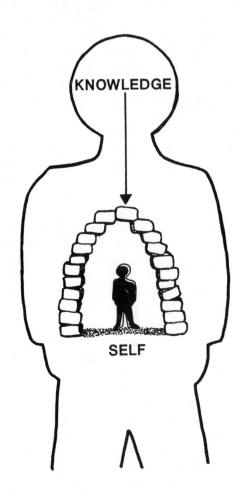

FIGURE 8

the stealth of the serpent in his home. In this illustration we see the lion and bear symbolize our extrinsic enemies, while the snake in the wall represent an intrinsic enemy attacking us through our personality.

As before, the walls represent our personality, and here the enemy has the greatest opportunity to disrupt a relationship, a marriage, a family, a church and even a society. Understanding who we are and how we function can help our personality serve us, rather than our being enslaved to our own unsteady personalities. Some personalities become brick-bound, and the person within is no more than a prisoner behind the walls of his heart, as illustrated in Figure 8. For many Christians there is tragic truth in the words of the comic strip character Pogo: "We have found the enemy, and he is us!"

As each of our negative responses becomes habitual, another brick is added to the wall. It is even possible for us to be so traumatized emotionally we actually wall off a section of our lives, determining no one will have opportunity to hurt us again. This wall may afford some degree of protection, but it also locks up part of our personality, affecting our ability to love, trust and form meaningful relationships. If a sizable portion of personality is locked away, then the symptoms become more severe, and it's more difficult to know who we are and why we react the way we do. This dynamic may also make us susceptible to allowing a platform of deception to grip our lives, binding us up and keeping us from being free to develop who we are.

The Scripture says that as we know the Truth,

the Truth will make us free.[10] The more truth that comes into our lives, the freer we become to live as God intended.

CONCLUSION

In this chapter we have seen how the walls we build to protect ourselves may actually imprison and rob our lives of their very essence. *If we are not to build walls and depend on them for security, how then do we defend ourselves against the storms that would devastate not only our walls, but our very beings?* We will answer this important question in the ensuing chapters.

---

10. John 8:32

CHAPTER FOUR

SOUR GRAPES

"The parents ate sour grapes and the children had the bitter taste."

- An old Israeli proverb -

In the previous chapter on deception and storms, we saw how false prophets proclaim we need to build walls to protect us from the storms of life. One of the false prophet categories we mentioned was parents and their great influence over the paths of their children.

The above proverb[1] looks at the same process but from another perspective. The sour grapes relate to the sins of the fathers and the sour effects they leave on successive generations.[2] Through the prophet Ezekiel, God commanded Israel to cease using this proverb, as it had become an excuse not to take personal responsibility. In other words, Israel blamed its forefathers for their sins, but God held each individual accountable.

---

1. Ezekiel 18:2
2. Numbers 14:18

In order to understand further what God is saying, let's review some United States military research[3] gathered from 200 children ages three to eighteen. The research team of psychologists and sociologists validated a "father-deficit" syndrome in the children whose fathers were absent due to being in the military. They found that the children's early reaction to their father's departure resembled reactions of those who lose a father by death. The team tabulated some of the most frequent symptoms recorded in the surveys, as follows:

RAGE
DENIAL AND FANTASY
REUNION ATTEMPTS
GUILT
FEAR
IMPULSE CHANGES
REGRESSION

As I contemplated this data, I found myself linking these infantile responses with some of the major pathological symptoms in our society. Suppose the reactions above were never resolved and the children continued in their struggle on through to adulthood?

For example, the U.S. military keeps a father away on active duty for six months at a time with only brief interludes at home.

The child first feels hurt through separation. He may either supress and internalize or externalize his hurt in *rage*. Internalizing greatly predisposes to emotional illness, while externalizing may lead to social illness. The temper tantrums of early child-

---

3. a) Armand M. Nicholi II M.D.: "Fractured Family," <u>Christianity Today</u>, May 25, 1979, p. 10.   b) Archives of General Psychiatry.

hood may be replaced with episodes of crime and violence in later life.

RAGE ————————————➤ CRIME

Denial and fantasy, the second reaction in the list, may also result when the hurt of separation becomes unbearable. The child then denies the separation, fantasizing conversations and meetings with his father. This may predispose him to a platform of self-deception, as well as the development of one or several of the many personality disorders.

DENIAL & FANTASY ————➤ PERSONALITY DISORDERS

Another response seen among the children was attempts at *reunion* with their absent fathers. Over and over, like a broken record, they pestered their mothers about daddy's return. No matter how often mother explained the date and time of daddy's return, the plea would start all over again. "When is daddy coming home?" Finally mother's resistance would crumble leaving her exasperated and frustrated.

Such a constant attempt at reunion is clearly due to the absence of the important father-child relationship. Sensing that lack, those children may live out their past in future adult relationships by grasping at what relationships they do have. As they grow up and continue to wrestle in attempts at reunion, their personalities may be distorted by possessiveness.

This distortion may be seen in many marriages

where a wife wants to know every detail of her husband's schedule, or where a husband becomes paranoid about losing his wife. Out of fear he demands to know the details of all her activities. Where there has been wounding or rejection, the tendency is to become possessive in our relationships at any level. However, when we possess a relationship, we also asphyxiate it.

REUNION ATTEMPTS ⟶ POSSESSIVENESS

Feelings of *guilt* may be false or real on the part of the child whose father is absent. He may blame himself for the absence, or may think or feel that he is unworthy, undeserving, inferior and even unlovable. Such guilt is a heavy yoke for a child to grow up with, and I believe it is a major contribution to more serious forms of depression.

The child's guilt may also be increased and compounded by his bad behavior, coupled with his mother's inability to cope without the father's moral support and discipline. If discipline is absent or inadequate, then the child's guilt is unrelieved and the unacceptable behavior increases.

GUILT ⟶ REBELLION

Next the guilt-laden child may begin to discipline himself, possibly resulting in masochism. This self-punishment can relieve his guilt and ease his drive toward rebellion, but then we see the following reactions:

GUILT INTERNALIZED ⟶ DEPRESSION

GUILT EXTERNALIZED ⟶ DELINQUENCY

Next the children of absentee fathers evidenced *fear* by clinging possessively to their mothers and screaming inordinately. To them, Mother is the last remaining element of security, and should never be out of sight! Such unresolved fears fill the lives of people in both the developed and underdeveloped parts of the world.

Tranquilizers and hypnotics are all too often used in a vain attempt to deal with the rising tide of neuroses. People are popping pills to assist them to sleep, wake, eat more, eat less, have more energy, and on it goes.

The Bible warns that men's hearts will fail them for fear.[4] We can see all around us how the element of sustained anxiety and tension in our lives predisposes us to heart problems and a multiplicity of other conditions.

FEAR ────────────────▶ NEUROSES

Impulse changes can be defined as responses in our bodies resulting from internalizing unresolved stress on a continual basis. The researchers observed this in infants who had already achieved bladder and bowel control yet made a retrograde step. Other older children also began to wet the bed at night, much to their embarrassment and mother's chiding. Still other children gulped their food down like animals. All these examples show the stressed internal environment affecting bodily functions. Perhaps this is why today, general practitioners encounter up to 80% of their patients with psychosomatic elements to their problems. All too often only symptoms are being dealt with, and the

---

4. Luke 21:26

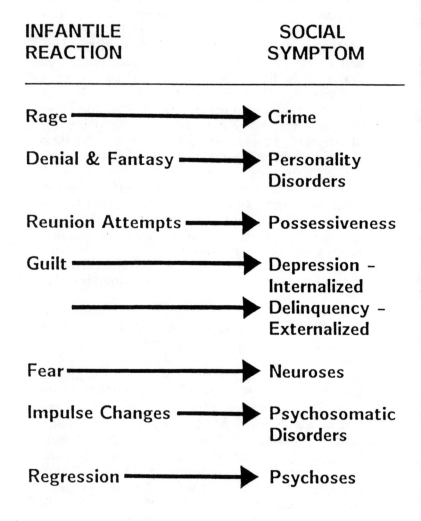

INFANTILE REACTION	SOCIAL SYMPTOM
Rage ——————→	Crime
Denial & Fantasy ——→	Personality Disorders
Reunion Attempts ——→	Possessiveness
Guilt ——————→	Depression – Internalized
——————→	Delinquency – Externalized
Fear ——————→	Neuroses
Impulse Changes ——→	Psychosomatic Disorders
Regression ————→	Psychoses

FIGURE 9

precipitating lifestyle goes on unchallenged and un-changed.

IMPULSE CHANGES ⟶ PSYCHOSOMATIC DISORDERS

Regression was observed in the children studied when the trauma of the separation was so great they withdrew from active participation in life's major functions, namely, eating, playing, socializing and the like. Some children withdrew into a corner and curled up in a ball, assuming a fetal position. The message this sends is of deep fear and insecurity, and it resulted in a desire to regress to the relative safety of the fetal stage within the womb.

In situations of sustained trauma or repeated episodes, these children may become psychotic, op-ting for a world of fantasy rather than painful reality.

REGRESSION ⟶ PSYCHOSES

If we evaluate the social symptoms shown in Figure 9, we can see the major challenges in social development today are all listed. From this, we can draw the conclusion that unresolved conflicts in the inner child may lock the adult into immature pat-terns of behavior.

The apostle Paul addresses this issue when he says, "You have been on the bottle too long. Grow up! I desire that you leave off milk and begin to eat meat."[5]

Psychologists, psychiatrists and other therapists all recognize that the great challenge in society is to

---

5. 1 Corinthians 3:1-2; (Paraphrase mine).

help grown-ups be "grown up," both internally and externally. The inner child can be enjoyed, but to enthrone it is wrong.

The military research we have reviewed relates only to the *absent* father. Imagine if the father was an alcoholic and abusive to his family, or suppose he was openly immoral and unfaithful. The consequent negative, depreciating input into the child's life could be even more traumatic and possibly chain him to childishness for the rest of his life. The same effect may also result from a deficit in motherhood, particularly in infancy.

The sour grapes then represent parental problems or failures and the bitter taste is that which influences and affects the child adversely in his own development.

The Bible describes this process as the sins of the parents being visited on the third and fourth generation,[6] reflecting what we currently call "familial patterns" in sociopathology. The issue brings up a popular controversy: is nature or nurture to blame? Is the problem inherited, or acquired? If it is acquired, the problem can be changed and accountability would be in order.

The military research also indicates some of the major stimuli to wall building, as well as reactions to parenting that wounds. God's antidote to this bitter tasting toxin is seen in Psalm 103:17.

> *"But the mercy and lovingkindness of the Lord are from everlasting to everlasting upon those who reverently and worshipfully fear Him, and His righteousness is to children's children."*[7]

---

6. Numbers 14:18
7. Psalm 103:17, Amplified Bible

God desires sweet grapes and a sweet taste in the children's mouths. He wants His salvation, His lovingkindness and His righteousness to be passed on by parents to their children and on to the children's children. This is His proverb and His plan! If parents will turn back to God and embrace His ways, they will then begin to invoke His blessing on their descendants.

Rejection may be passed on from one generation to another, either willfully or blindly. If we go back to our original thought we could depict it this way:

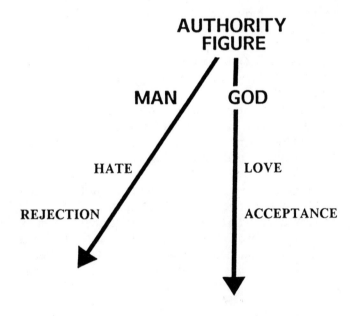

AUTHORITY FIGURE

MAN **GOD**

HATE LOVE

REJECTION ACCEPTANCE

From the figure, we see that with God as our authority figure, we receive love and acceptance, but when we put man in that place, we often experience masked or open hate and rejection. The factor separating the "human plumbline" from the "divine plumbline" we will call the LOVE DEFICIT. The line of love and acceptance is the divine plumbline's position, representing God's disposition and desire toward us. The line of hate and rejection is a human plumbline position by which sinful man builds his life, instead of following the divine plumbline. The angle between the human and divine plumblines could be represented in terms of a "love deficit." The greater this angle, the greater the lack of God's kind of love.

To consider some of the effects of the love deficit, let's look at a little biblical mathmatics:

YOU MINUS LOVE = ?

What is your answer to the above equation? Can you answer without qualifying love? Love is such a loose term these days it applies to anything, from loving your dog to loving God!

For our usage, let's define love from the Greek word *agape*, meaning such a great commitment and loyalty to someone, one is willing to lay down his life for him. This is love in its highest form, a kind we all need in our lives. The greater the love deficit a person has, the closer they feel to being like a zero. They feel deeply as though life has very little value, if any at all.

YOU MINUS LOVE = ZERO

Being loved gives us a sense of self-value

and having worth in life. Unloved people, used people, abused people, rejected people and broken up people all wrestle with a low sense of self-worth.

Love is often mistakenly used synonymously with lust. While lust involves getting pleasure from someone, love is just the opposite. Love involves a giving and sharing of one's life, to enhance the well being and produce the highest in another. The catchword for lust is, "Give me!" while for love it is, "I give you." We could alter the equation to the following:

$$YOU\ PLUS\ LUST = ZERO$$

Often people try to balance the love deficit in their lives with a lust credit. For example, an unloved son goes into the world seeking the love he needs by having multiple sexual affairs, or perhaps an unloved daughter gives her body to men in her attempt to balance her love deficit. Yet in both cases, all they would receive is lust and their love deficit goes unchanged.

LOVE DEFICIT DEMONSTRATED

Gita was an attractive young woman with auburn hair and brown eyes, but I immediately noticed her apparent inability to look anyone in the eyes. Instead she kept her head bowed to the floor, and a sadness seemed to emanate from her.

After listening to the teaching on *The Divine Plumbline*, Gita was one of many, who during our two days of ministry, came forward for prayer. She sat on the edge of the chair with her head down and hair cascading over her face. Tears

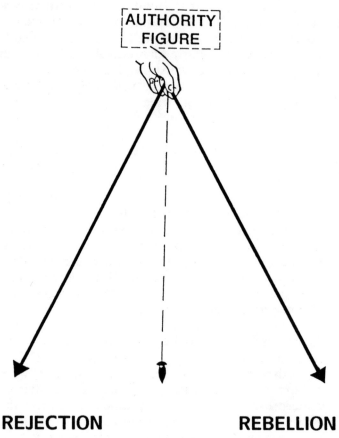

REJECTION   **REBELLION**

FIGURE 10

started making a puddle in her lap as her shoulders shook with uncontrollable sobs. I had to strain to hear her words as she slowly began to share.

Gita explained she had no relationship with her parents, who were successful professional people always expecting her to follow in their steps. As she grew up, her parents never gave her any physical affection beyond an odd peck on the cheek from time to time. The real affection she enjoyed came from her relationship with her doll. She lavished it with love for hours, until the doll grew more and more soiled and ragged.

One day, Gita said, her Dad came into her room with shocking news.

"Your mother and I have been talking," he began. "We want to get you a new doll and throw this one away."

Horrified, she clung to her doll, screaming, "No! I don't want a new doll!"

One night Gita's dad came into her room while she slept. Taking her doll and leaving a new one in its place, he threw her treasure into the incinerator. When she awoke the next morning, she was devastated. She never touched the new doll or wanted anything to do with it.

The incident only further alienated Gita from her parents. As a teenager she began to look for love in the wrong places. After a series of affairs, Gita found herself on a fast track leading to a life of prostitution. Now she was left destitute, engulfed in loneliness, and desperately needed to hear from the Lord.

As we waited before the Lord together, I received a revelation: Gita had actually become the little doll in search of love. As I told her this, she began to weep. Then the Lord gave me more words for her.

"God is adopting you as His little doll," I told

her. "He is going to love you even more than you loved your doll."

Then, instead of weeping in a broken and hurt way, Gita's tears turned to ones of joy as the love of the Father overwhelmed her. From that point on, her life began to take on a new frame of reference.

Living a life style of lust in an attempt to satisfy our desires only enhances both the love deficit and a feeling of worthlessness. If one's life is of no worth or value, why live it? Gita followed a human plumbline of rejection which emerged as the reference point for her life, and she remained passive, expecting rejection.

But suppose we do not accept the feelings of rejection as a way of life? In that case we may find ourselves beginning to follow another human plumbline of rebellion.

AUTHORITY FIGURE

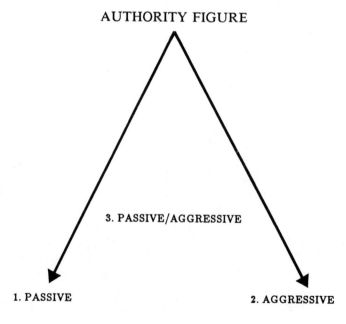

3. PASSIVE/AGGRESSIVE

1. PASSIVE

2. AGGRESSIVE

When rebellion emerges, a person takes an aggressive stance, striving to disprove the message of rejection and inferiority he has lived under so long. Yet others may be passive/aggressive types who swing back and forth from rejection to rebellion according to the suitability of the occasion. Hence we have three potential response patterns, as seen in the figure on page 68.

When these three responses become life-long habit patterns, they may form the basis of developing certain personality distortions in the individual. When this happens, each distortion forms a building block for the walls to be built in our hearts. In the next chapter, we will continue our study of the imagery from the book of Amos as we uncover more of the intrigue behind these walls.

CHAPTER FIVE

WALLS OF DEFENSE
REJECTION

In Amsterdam, alleys and byways form a narrow, intimate maze presided over by houses of every shape and size. Recently, while walking down some of those byways, a Dutch friend pointed to a row of houses leaning precariously. Some slanted so severely they had to be propped because houses next to them had been demolished. In some situations these quaint constructions leaned out of plumb by as much as six feet between top and bottom.

We have already seen how God portrayed to Amos a picture of His people being like a wall out of line, just like those leaning walls in Amsterdam. In the human personality, prolonged rejection may precipitate a severe psychological distortion as great as those walls I saw in Amsterdam. We will proceed to examine these distortions in a brick by brick study.

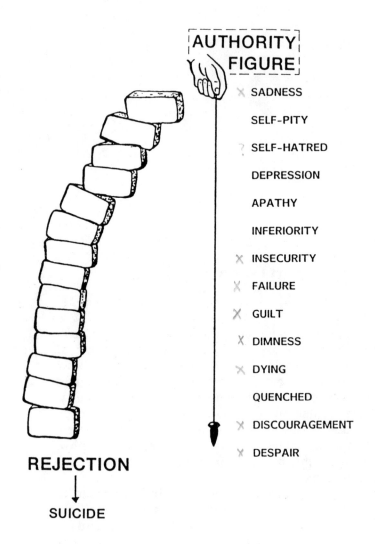

FIGURE 11

EMOTIONS

We will let each building block represent both a blockage to God's planned personality development, as well as a block in the walls of our hearts. In the following list of blocks, mark an asterisk where you find yourself identifying. This will later be helpful as we consider keys to change. The first category of personality distortions relate to a very strong influence in our lives - our emotions.

SADNESS

We can define sadness as "sorrowful, mournful, showing or causing sorrow."[1] Sometimes this emotion can cast a shadow over the entire personality, as was the case with Mark.

Tall and slim, with a shock of blond hair and deep blue eyes, Mark had a sad countenance darkening his otherwise striking appearance. I had the opportunity to counsel him for several hours, and I found the reason for his apparent grief. As a young man, Mark had been so skilled a runner, he had the potential to represent his country in the Olympics. All his drives were focused on obtaining this goal until he became involved with a girl. Soon after they married, Mark's bride objected to the long hours of training, and pressured him to quit until he gave up his dream to save the marriage. Not long after, Mark discovered his wife had been unfaithful to him. This, along with the disappointment of not being an Olympic runner, left him with a deep-seated grief.

People may normally be sad over a brief period

---

1. The Concise Oxford Dictionary of Current English, (Oxford:University Press, 1954).

of time, for example from the loss of a spouse in mid-life, but, when someone becomes repeatedly dysfunctional for longer and longer periods of time, a chronic state of grief has emerged. Such an unhealthy, sustained grief is often the result of a failure to release from one's spirit the loss of a dream or perhaps a failed expectation. From Mark's story, it was clear he had not done this, and his sustained grief robbed him of life's fulfillment and joy.

The Bible describes this sadness as a garment of mourning.[2] Over the years, I have ministered to many like Mark who have utilized the block of sadness to build up their walls. Other examples include a young girl who lost her virginity through incest; a wife who lost her husband's love due to his unfaithfulness; and a young woman desiring to become a doctor who wasn't accepted into medical school. In cases like these, sadness is a substitute emotion in response to sustained blows of rejection from a significant source.

In times of grief, we need to turn to God the Father, the source of true comfort for sadness. When Mark returned to my office, we prayed for the release of his grief. As he surrendered this to God, he began to experience a release of his underlying emotions and received God's comfort and healing.

SELF-PITY

Self-pity is not only a bad habit, it's also a sin. The more we indulge in it, the easier it is to shift into this thinking pattern whenever disagreeable circumstances confront us. A person practicing

---

2. Isaiah 61:3

self-pity is continually consoling himself over some disappointment. When it becomes overwhelming, he looks to others to console him as well, manipulating them into feeding his self-pity. Soon he is in a bottomless pit no one can fill, failing to face up to the conflict and resolve it. Such self-pity not only exhibits rejection, it enhances it. Yet it is usually not easily seen by the one ensnared. True thanksgiving is a sure biblical exercise for the healing of chronic self-pity and negative introspection.

SELF-HATRED

An amazing number of people in this 20th century struggle with negative feelings about themselves. For some it is sporadic, but for others this struggle is chronic and crippling.

Self-hatred can be defined as rejecting oneself after being rejected by others. Helping an individual overcome self-hatred may well be one of the greatest challenges a counselor will ever face.

The first time I met Inez, I was impressed by her bright personality. Before attending one of our counseling schools in Youth With A Mission, she had been involved in a rehabilitation counseling ministry. Now, during a three month counseling course Inez was among about 30 students from around the world who had come not only to learn counseling skills, but to become whole people themselves.

ROOTS OF SELF-HATRED

Several weeks into the course, Inez suddenly went into deep depression. Unable to sleep at night, she began to hear voices, and gradually slipped into an acute anxiety state. Inez met with two staff members regularly, but refused to let anyone through the walls she hid behind. As we kept trying to reach her, little by little she began to share the deep, wounding experiences she suffered as a child. For the first time, she began to express the pain she felt living behind those walls.

Inez explained that when she was just a young teenager, her father arranged for her to be coached regularly in tennis by her uncle. Gradually, over the weeks he began to molest her, and the emotions that surfaced were so powerful, Inez didn't know how to deal with them. She felt unable to tell her parents, convinced they would never believe her. Besides deeply resenting her uncle, Inez also wrestled with resentment towards her father for sending her with him in the first place. Towards herself, Inez felt guilt, uncleanness and self-hate.

The staff of the school regularly interceded for

her in prayer, until one day, during a time of ministry in class, Inez went forward for prayer. Now everyone's attention focused on her, as she stood silently before us, clenching and unclenching her hands. Obviously struggling with some internal battle, suddenly Inez began speaking slowly and deliberately to the class.

"I hate it here!" she said emphatically. "I hate you! I have feelings of hate towards God. I hate myself! I hate my parents!"

After this outburst, Inez just stood there as we absorbed the meaning of her words in shocked silence. All was still, but for a few muffled sobs in the class. The rest of us just prayed and looked to God for His direction.

A KEY TO RELEASE

Then a young man called Derek came to me, whispering something he felt God was prompting him to do and asking for confirmation. Sensing it was right, I told him to go ahead.

Standing before Inez in front of the class, Derek said, "I want to stand in for your dad and ask your forgiveness. Will you forgive me?"

Inez just looked at him with a cold, unresponsive face, apparently masking any feeling.

"Will you forgive me?" Derek asked again.

Silence.

When for the third time Derek requested forgiveness and she still gave no response, he began to sob, greatly feeling God's broken heart toward His wounded daughter.

In hushed silence, the class interceded until at last Inez broke the silence. "Dad, I forgive you," she said haltingly. There was a long pause.

Then she spoke again. "Dad, will you forgive me for the hatred I've had toward you?"

As she spoke those releasing words she crumbled into the arms of the young student, releasing cleansing tears to wash away all the resentment, bitterness and hatred that had formed a wall in her heart for so many years. As Inez went on to express forgiveness toward her family and herself, receiving the forgiveness of God, her self-hatred dissipated. By the end of the term most of her symptoms were gone.

Later Inez wrote me the following words:
"On the day I was ministered to in front of the class by Derek, the Lord took me to Isaiah 38:15-16. It became very clear to me that my insomnia was due to bitterness toward my dad, which I had tried to cover up all my life. I had become very deceptive, particularly with my emotions, so that how I related to people on the outside was quite contrary to how I felt about them on the inside. The Lord told me that the key to release was an honest confession of my heart's real feelings about people and life, hence the expression of hatred I expressed that day."

Over the following months, Inez continued to change dramatically as she began feeling more and more of the love of God and His compassion for her. Upon returning home, Inez was reconciled to her father and later had opportunities to minister to abused young people out of her experience.

Cases of incest like Inez are common today and play a large role in producing self-hatred. Just as in any lust, incest brings with it a depreciation of worth and value within the person unlike anything else. But with incest self-hatred is multiplied, because the person is betrayed by a family member.

The experience is so devaluating to a person, feelings of self-blame and resentment will arise, and if they go unchallenged, self-hatred is produced.

DEPRESSION

For many years depression has been the number one emotional illness in the U.S., and it's on the increase, particularly among the young. What is depression and how does it relate to God's plumbline? Depression in its simplest and most common form can best be explained in terms of how we may react to a loss.

We may first feel a general loss of vitality and energy, appearing tired and sad. Then we withdraw from social life, and even from close friends. Activity at work and at home may decline and everything seems gloomy and hopeless. Our thoughts may be few, and if any occur, they are dim. We have difficulty concentrating. Feelings of guilt are usual, with self-reproach and self-depreciation a close second. Insomnia often results.

It is normal to have some depressed feelings once in a while, but when they increase in frequency, and length, the person may need to take some remedial action. A simple but useful illustration is a car which begins to lose power. The engine coughs and splutters, and we obviously need to pull over and look under the hood to see what's wrong. Of course when our car's performance is depressed, we immediately see something is amiss and seek to put it right. But, when we ourselves become depressed, all too often the real message of our mood is silenced by an anti-depressant drug.

What is so often ignored is that depression in its simplest form is a mood message, indicating something needs to be rectified in our lives. Chemicals may alter our surface mood, but they won't touch our spirit. Most often, our lifestyle is what really needs to change to prevent a relapse.

Just as joy is a symptom of life, so depression is a symptom of something dying or missing within. Sometimes biochemical ingredients may be missing and need to be replaced in organic or hereditary disorders affecting the mood, but such organic causes account for just over 5% of mental illness today. Depression can be a very complex mixture of physical and mental factors, and thus difficult to treat. However if we fail to evaluate the lifestyle of the depressed person, we fail that person.

APATHY

Defined as "passionless existence; indolence of mind, or without feeling,"[3] apathy is an arch enemy of life. In fact, it's the first stage in giving up the challenge of life itself. The Bible speaks about many slumbering in the faith,[4] and a series of setbacks and discouragements can provide a platform for this evil elixir of the enemy. Because of the church's apathy and failure to shine it's light and be the salt of the earth, the world has instead been invading the church. At times it's even difficult to distinguish between the church and the world.

One day upon walking into Lydia's house I received not only a quick education in how to create a mess, but I saw what can happen when apathy gets hold of a person. The counter top was stacked with dirty dishes, and books, clothes, and shoes were strewn everywhere. Dust caked every available surface, and in the midst of the chaos sat Lydia - disheveled and unkempt, watching TV.

---

3. The Concise Oxford Dictionary, op. cit.
4. Romans 11:8

"Look at her, she's been like this for days," her distraught husband howled. "She just doesn't seem to care about anything."

Such apathy arises out of thoughts and feelings of rejection and failure: "What's the use! It will never work," we moan. "I'll always be like this!"

INTELLECT

This second category of blocks in the walls we build relates more to our thinking process and resulting attitudes. Continue to mark the blocks that apply to your own life.

INFERIORITY

"No man who says, 'I'm as good as you,' believes it. He would not say it if he did. The St. Bernard never says it to the toy dog, nor the scholar to the dunce ... What it expresses is precisely the itching, smarting, writhing awareness of an inferiority ... "

C.S. Lewis - *The Screwtape Letters*

The intellect is one of Satan's greatest psychological playgrounds. The gut-level feeling of inferiority shackles many an intellect, paralyzing the ability to think clearly. A mistaken conclusion people often draw from recurrent rejection in their lives is that they are in fact inferior. Once they have concluded the worst, they then make up phony reasons why they are inferior to fit this misbegotten conclusion. "I'm too fat," or "I'm too skinny," " I'm too small," "I'm too tall," "I have too big a nose," "I'm too dumb," and the reasons go on and on.

I also had developed a deep sense of inferiority, as a result of the humiliating classroom experience I mentioned in chapter one. Because the teacher showed me up as one of the few who couldn't tell time, I concluded I was inferior to the rest of the students. In oder to reduce my own vulnerability, I began withdrawing from almost all participation in the class, and it was many years before I understood why I preferred this passive observation, feeling threatened whenever participation was unavoidable.

All too often we allow ourselves to be convinced of our inferiority for whatever reason, and so become easy prey for intimidation by the enemy. Inferiority and unbelief are teammates out to destroy our confidence. Together they rob us of the victories that faith would otherwise have won.

INSECURITY

In today's society, insecurity is rampant, resulting from such factors as the epidemic of fractured and dysfunctional families. Insecurity is a direct result of the love deficit and the messages of rejection we receive in childhood. By contrast, security is directly related to love. Research has shown that children raised in environments lacking in love often experience deep-seated senses of insecurity. Some examples of this include an unwanted pregnancy, an undesirable gender, parents who are too busy or preoccupied with their own lives, or parents who are authoritarian and strict, with little warmth or affirmation. These are only a few of the examples that can predispose insecurity in an individual.

FAILURE

The words to a popular tune go as follows: "You're no good, no good, no good, no good. Baby, you're no good, no good, no good."

Sadly this message reminds me of how the father of one of my childhood friends spoke to him. One of the most common struggles for people living in rejection, is belief in a deep sense of their own unworthiness. They have a continuous feeling of inadequacy, with an inner voice saying, "I'm no good. I'll never amount to anything. Everything I do is wrong."

Many people are obsessed with the fear of failure, and when they do fail, they seem unable to recover and learn from the experience. Instead, they fall apart, pre-programed to believe the words they were told as children.

Words have incredible power to build us up or tear us down. Because we failed at something when we were young, we may have been labeled, "a failure." This label may grow with us and confirm the negative programming in our lives. The more we fail, the more we are convinced we are a failure. We then begin to put ourselves beyond even the grace of God.

GUILT

Is guilt a terrible liability, or a valuable asset? Should we embrace it, or repel it? The following simple illustration may bring some insight to this question:

Imagine you are driving through lush, beautiful countryside, back-dropped with snow-peaked mountains. Suddenly your attention is caught by a flashing red light on your dashboard. Trying to ignore it you drive on, hoping it will stop. For the next few miles it continues to flash, and your level of irritation mounts. Finally, in frustration, you reach into the glove box, remove a hammer and smash the little red flashing light! Free of this disturbance, you drive on, enjoying the feast of nature spread before you. But suddenly, your engine goes totally dead.

The red light represents our "guilt-o-meter," a built in warning system to save us from suffering and even death. It could flash on at any time of the day or night, mostly night when distraction and defenses are lowered by fatigue. We then have the option of either silencing it through suppression, diversion or coercion, or heeding its message, pulling over and evaluating our lifestyle.

The theories of Freudian psychology attempted to suppress guilt by turning down the sensitivity of the "guilt-o-meter." Freud believed the Super Ego and its messages to the Ego and Id, were mostly idealistic parent messages. No one could possibly attain to its standards. This idea has spawned many popular notions, resulting in a society flooded with so many people either wrestling with depression, or with rebellion over repressed guilt. But, if guilt's message is accurately received and understood, and appropriate adjustments are made, a life can return to balance and be enjoyed. Here is the great value of guilt when it's real, responded to correctly and understood maturely. Such guilt provides important guide posts and direction for life.

SPIRIT

The final category of personality development blocks belongs to that part of man through which he relates to the noumenal or unseen spirit world. The New Age movement with its new consciousness, new thought and other associated streams have brought to the forefront a fresh emphasis on man as a spiritual being. Medicine in its holistic movement is putting out feelings in search of spiritual resources and power for healing.

Dr. Elizabeth Kubler-Ross, an internationally recognized authority in death and dying, is using research with mediums to further her knowledge. While these methods are misguided, the hunger for the spiritual is certainly evident.

At last the spirit of man has come into fresh focus after decades of rationalistic skepticism. The Bible, the most ancient and trustworthy of all the documentaries on the spirit of man, states the following: "The Spirit of man (that factor in the human personality which proceeds immediately from God) is the lamp (candle) of the Lord, searching all his innermost parts."[5]

The picture of the candle is apt and useful in this context. When an individual identifies with a plumbline of rejection instead of the plumbline of God, he begins to live in this tilted position and his spirit is adversely affected.

When my wife and I worked as medical missionaries in West Africa, we discovered a condition which our medication could not cure. Young men in the prime of life would just lie down and die without any discernible disease. At our request our interpreter researched several of these young men's

5. Proverbs 20:27

backgrounds, and explained that in each case a powerful witch doctor had placed a curse on them, causing them to die on a certain day.

What happened during this time in their spirits could be described in terms of the candle and its flame. As each young man received and believed his fate, the "flame of his candle" grew dim and began to die out. Finally, as predicted the flame was quenched.

This illustration points to three blocks in the rejection wall:

DIMNESS . . .

DYING . . .

QUENCHED!

I have observed a similar process in hospital patients. Some refuse to die, while others go through the above sequence without even a fight.

I have seen over and over, that if people accept rejection repeatedly, they begin to think they are rejectable. Feelings quickly confirm this belief until finally they become bound in the spirit. Hope falters, and ...

DISCOURAGEMENT sets in. To illustrate this block, let me tell a story. One day the enemy set up a stall in a market to sell some of his wares. The highest price tag hung from a strange looking instrument. When asked what it was for, Satan replied, "Discouragement. This is my most powerful tool. I keep working on man with this, until finally he is drawn to ..."

DESPAIR! Laughing gleefully Satan continued unveiling his plot. "Once a man is in despair, he's no match for me! Instead, he becomes my prisoner and slave. How I love to lead Christians into despair over their ministries, their families, their finances and even their whole lives. A little push, and in time, their opposition to my kingdom gives way to eternity."

John Bunyan in his immortal Christian classic *Pilgrim's Progress* vividly describes the plight of Christian and Hopeful when they fall into the hands of Giant Despair. The two pilgrims are imprisoned by the giant in a dark stinking dungeon, and after beating them, he advises them to take their lives.

"Why should you choose life, seeing it is attended with so much bitterness?" he scoffs.

REASONS FOR DESPAIR

It was late at night and I was yawning on my way to bed when the phone rang.

"Bruce come quickly! Dion is in jail!" Instantly I was wide awake with shock and unbelief. Dion was not only a member of a local church, he was a dear friend. As I frantically threw on some clothes and got ready to dash to the police station, I couldn't help feeling there must be some mistake.

After meeting some church leaders down at the police station, they filled me in on Dion's arrest. Over the years Dion's wife had confided in me about his homosexual tendencies. Sure enough, two police decoys had trapped Dion in a public place and then charged him with intent to commit a felony. (In the country where this took place the practice of homosexuality was a felony.)

We were able to get Dion released that night, and as he "limped" toward us with shoulders hunched and head down, he looked like a broken man. Despair was written all over his face.

The following week two of us began to meet with Dion on a regular basis. Due to his self-condemnation and the humiliation of being caught, Dion had slipped into the pits of despair and depression. The local newspaper then splashed a sordid story about the incident that caused him to sink so low, all he could think about was suicide.

Day after day, a friend and I went to Dion's place to sit and pray with him. At first we felt like Job's friends who didn't know what to say or where to start, so they remained silent for seven days in grief and empathy for Job.[6]

However, unlike Job's friends, when we did open our mouths we had a case for sin and repentance to present. Dion's sin was already public. Our greatest battle was with his deep-seated self-pity and unrelenting self-condemnation. He was convinced he had committed the unpardonable sin and it was only a matter of time until hell would welcome him into its eternal torment.

Unable to talk him out of his suicidal position, we resorted to more intensive prayer with him. One morning, as we continued our vigil, we received some encouragement. We had been praying with Dion for about an hour when we noticed he began to sob in a different way. These were not tears of self-pity as before, but tears of relief and release. Suddenly it was as if he was seeing himself in a totally different light.

"Abba Father," (Dear Daddy) he sobbed at last.

---

6. Job 2:11-13

After that time, God in His grace and mercy began to meet with him, fanning the flame of the candle of his dim spirit once again. It was the start of Dion's coming out of a life of lust and perversion into one of love and truth.

After that day, we had much pain to help him walk through over the next few months, but the major victory had been won. With his lust addiction in remission, Dion's love relationship with God grew day by day. He began to enjoy spending time in prayer and meditation on the scriptures.

Then God gave him a revelation. Before, he had been serving God out of a sense of duty, as a slave serves his master, instead of serving God out of devotion, as service between a son and his father. Before his relationship with God had been coldly theological. He had a theology, which he taught well intellectually, but he hadn't had an emotionally vibrant love for God. Over the months we began to see that vitality restored as he discovered *Abba Father*.

CONCLUSION

Following a human plumbline of rejection is a great handicap and, if allowed, could rob us even of life itself. The more aggressive individual may resist passively accepting rejection and adopt a new reactionary reference point by following a human plumbline of rebellion. To completely resist following the rejection plumbline may open the way to accept rebellion. In the next chapter, we will take a closer look at this dilemma.

COME ASIDE

Review the blocks you marked with an asterisk.

Ponder the extenuating circumstances that caused these blocks to be added to your walls.

Does their influence still affect you at times?

What can you do to change these distortions?

CHAPTER 6

WALLS OF DEFENSE
REBELLION

Idi Amin Dada, the previous ruler of Uganda, is a contemporary example of a man with a classic rebellious personality in the most extreme form. Growing up as a member of the Nubians, an itinerant group, Idi Amin continually moved from place to place with his mother, never knowing who his real father was. In Uganda the Nubians are considered the lowliest of the low. The message he received while growing up was clearly one of rejection.

When Amin joined the military and rose in rank, he threw off the message of rejection he had received all his life and began following a plumbline of rebellion. He developed a superiority complex, over-compensating for his humble origin and poor education. He became a fanatical soldier, ruthlessly competitive and willing to use any means

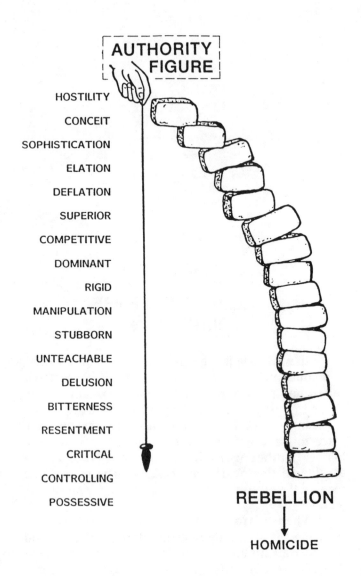

FIGURE 12

to further his political ambitions. Emulating his hero, Adolph Hitler, Amin was responsible for the torture and murder of over 100,000 of his own people since 1971.

Amin's hostility was especially apparent in the grossly sadistic way he tortured his "enemies" before throwing them to crocodiles. His controlling grip and utter possessiveness was also seen in his absolute determination to succeed by brute strength, cunning and falsehood.

In addition, Amin's personal conceit knew no bounds. On many occasions he wrote to the Queen of England offering to help solve the political and economic problems of the United Kingdom. He even invited himself to become Advisor to the Queen! He became so defensive of his authority that he was unable to deal with anyone even questioning his power. He developed a "rule by decree," and anyone who challenged or disagreed with him was put to death. It was the only way Amin knew to silence those who questioned his authority.

Amin is quoted as saying, "I, myself, consider myself the most powerful figure in the world," thus displaying his delusions of grandeur, accompanied by a spirit of domination, manipulation, stubbornness and unteachableness.

EMOTIONS

We will now look at the wall of rebellion block by block. Following the pattern of the previous study on the wall of rejection, mark an asterisk alongside those blocks with which you identify. We will begin with the blocks relating to the emotions.

HOSTILITY

During counseling in Japan with a middle-aged man, the subject of his fathering surfaced. Suddenly he leapt up from his seat, and with an ear piercing shout, he smashed his fist down on the table, almost breaking it in half with a karate chop. Just talking about his father had caused a deep-seated hurt to rise in the form of hostility. Anger had not only blocked his deep hurt, but also his personality development.

Anger can be released in a constructive way, but unharnessed hostility can be very dangerous. Anger often arises from hurt, and if hurt is incessant, anger may also be. A person with this persistent temper problem often suffers from some unresolved, internal conflict or an unhealed wound deep within. When anger finds no acceptable outlet it goes underground. It may become a vicious cycle of first over-controlling and then exploding out of control. With these individuals, so many emotions may accumulate that either deep depression or explosive anger becomes the only way out. When painful feelings are chronically suppressed, they may surface in the form of mental illness or psychosomatic disorders.

CONCEIT

This distortion is best defined as being aloof or apart from others, reflecting an overt degree of personal vanity and egocentricity. A conceited person usually struggles with loneliness, yet potential friendships are warded off by aloof behavior or condescending comments. People feel depreciated and even belittled through this expression of one-upmanship. This person's feelings of value and worth are strongly enhanced at the expense of others resulting in a loss of companionship.

SOPHISTICATION

This brick could sometimes be called "pseudo-sophistication." Achieving sophistication is often attempted by the conceited or egocentric individual. Coming from the word "sophism," which means a false argument intended to deceive, "sophistication" means to mislead so as to deprive a person or thing of inherent simplicity. It also means to tamper with, so as to adulterate or make artificial.[1]

Many of those I counsel who appear to be the most sophisticated, often turn out to be artificial or unreal. They appear to be together, smooth and in complete control, emanating an air of independence and self confidence, but beneath the surface they may suffer from insecurity, inferiority and phobias of one kind or another.

Conceit and this kind of pseudo-sophistication often result in real barriers to warm and loving relationships. First impressions of individuals often give us a gut level positive or negative response. Where do these gut feelings come from? Are they reliable? Let me explain how I think it works:

Often, when meeting a new person, I believe we have a flash-back on our cerebral computer to a similar person of the past. Our gut-level response to that person depends on whether the experience with that person from the past was warm and friendly or cold and wounding. If the memory is negative, we tend to ignore or avoid the person and so fail to develop a relationship. However, if the memory is positive, we readily move toward establishing a new relationship. But what we often fail

---

1. The Concise Oxford Dictionary, op. cit.

to recognize is that the most difficult relationship to develop is the one we most want to avoid. Yet, if we force ourselves to explore it, that relationship holds the greatest potential for healing and growth.

Where the internal computer fails in its feedback is in differentiating between the past and present persons. We tend to respond to our cerebral computer feedback as if it had the whole truth, but this example alone illustrates its fallibility. We must learn to update and reinterpret the old program.

ELATION and DEFLATION

In 1973, Joshua Logan, the extraordinarily talented director and producer in the American theater, spoke these words: "Depression is terrifying; and elation - its non-identical twin sister - is even more terrifying, attractive as she may be for the moment. But as she goes higher, man is in even more danger than when in the depths of the depression." Logan spoke these words before an American Medical Association symposium on depression, exposing his 30 year personal history of "bi-polar" manic to depressive mood swings.

Whenever conflict or pressure occurs, minor mood swings are common in life. A crisis along life's way is similar to a bump in the road. Just as a car's shock absorbers slide up and down, so do our moods. This is normal, and just as a car eventually settles down under a load, so do we - unless our tension level is extreme. In this event, our mood may swing up into a manic state or drop down into a depressive state. Or it may agitatedly vacillate between both states. These mood swings may become so severe they cause a breakdown of emotional control, or what is called psychosis. Rest and resolution of the inner conflict are important preventive measures.

INTELLECT

The second category I want to consider relates to our thinking process and its resulting attitudes. Continue to mark the blocks you identify with.

SUPERIOR

We see the block of superiority most commonly in the academic world, which in many instances has become a type of caste system. All too often, those with higher qualifications relate to lower ranks only on basic issues, if at all. But when people constantly act in a superior, condescending manner, it often indicates they are over-compensating for their own feelings of inferiority. When we are put down by them, they feel lifted up.

This air of one-upmanship is usually an attempt to mask and compensate for painful, repressed inferiority. Such feelings may have been programmed by abusive parenting, or early peer persecution, but this block of superiority very often isolates the individual from maintaining meaningful relationships in life.

COMPETITIVE

To the casual onlooker, Graham was in the prime of his life and ministry and seemed to have it all together. But in my office, he began to weep as he reflected over the years of energy and effort expended in church-related work. Exhausted and on the verge of burnout, he realized he had been competing for the love of people and even God throughout most of his life. How had he arrived at this place? What had predisposed him to such a stressful lifestyle?

This young man, like so many others, was raised in an environment where he was only accepted or affirmed if he performed well. His parents' conditional love demanded that certain standards were maintained, such as top grades at school and the highest performance in athletics and other areas of his life. Yet even at top performance, he received little or no affirmation and lots of criticism. When encouragement was given, it was only to stress that somehow he should have done better.

Over and over he had been told, "No son of mine will come home with grades like this!" The message clearly passed on was that unless he performed well enough, he would be rejected. But this kind of conditional love produces unreachable goals and unattainable standards in the minds of children. As a result of a similar upbringing, many adults today are performing for affirmation or love. Even a man's service to God can be an exhausting attempt to win a love that has already been given freely and fully and yet not received.

Some years ago the Lord began to show me the importance of affirming my sons, Michael and Lionel, during times when they were doing nothing other than being themselves. Seeing them playing on the floor with their Lego, a favorite pastime when they were young, or even just reading a book, I would put my arm around their shoulders and express my love and appreciation for who they are. Over the years, I've continued to do this. As they matured and developed into young men, I believe they received the message that Dad loves them for *who* they are, and not just for *what* they do.

DOMINANT

Today, more and more wives are not only playing the key role in their marriages, they are dominating the whole relationship. This pattern in contemporary marriages is of considerable interest and concern to sociologists.

What is causing this significant shift in the family? Such dominance arises out of insecurity, and insecurity comes from a love deficit. Husbands have either forgotten, or do not know, how to love their wives. Often they lust after them without understanding the difference between love and lust. So many times lust and love are used as synonyms, when they are actually closer to being antonyms, the opposite of each other. A lusting relationship leaves a wife feeling used and insecure, and as a result frustration and even frigidity may set in. In order to avoid this process, a wife may then try to manipulate her mate into meeting her need for love. Such domineering moves may eventually destroy a relationship, and that is exactly what is happening in so many families today.

RIGID

To be rigid means: "Not flexible, stiff, unyielding."[2] This personality distortion was clearly

---

2. The Concise Oxford Dictionary, op. cit.

evidenced by one young man in my class. During a discussion time after one of my lectures, he stood up and very eloquently began to expound his position. Around the room others made comments, but some openly disagreed with his views. Quietly watching the drama, I allowed the discussion to continue as I observed how he rigidly held onto his opinions no matter what they said. At last, in a raised voice, he made a last desperate bid, then stormed out of the room. Because his identity was so wrapped up in his ideas, the young man could not handle the crisis of being wrong. To accept that his idea was contrary to others opinions would be to see himself as wrong, totally depreciating his value or worth.

Others of us may put our security in a structure of one kind or another, at home or at work or school. Even the thought of change may cause us to over react, but such rigidity roadblocks our development. We can see this distortion in a husband who expresses such rigidity when his wife moves his favorite chair during spring cleaning. What is our own reaction when our favorite structures are moved or removed from our lives? Is our identity wrapped up in the familiarity of our surroundings?

STUBBORNNESS

A story is told in the Scriptures about a stubborn donkey,[3] but in the end the donkey's master, Balaam, proved to be the stubborn one. The master saddled his donkey early one morning and set out on a long journey. They hadn't traveled far when suddenly the donkey veered off the path into a field. Angrily, the master struck the donkey and

---

3. Numbers 22:22-33

tried to turn her back onto the path, but instead she thrust herself against a rock wall, crushing her master's foot. He struck her again angrily, but he didn't know she was responding to an angel standing in the road with His sword drawn. Three times she swerved off the path to protect her master from being cut down and each time the master beat her. Finally, when she fell down with him on her back, he threatened to kill her. Suddenly, his eyes were opened and he saw the Angel of the Lord standing before him, sword still drawn.

Man's great stubbornness, as seen in this story of Balaam, is one of God's great battles. Stubbornness often results from our insecurity in a new situation, and the consequence is failure to trust God or obey Him. Stubbornness may also result from habit patterns developed over a period of time, especially habit patterns directed toward authority figures who have misused or abused their position.

UNTEACHABLENESS

Some people find it difficult to acknowledge learning something new. To do so would mean a put down of self, since much of their identity is wrapped up in their knowledge. Instead of adapting to challenges in life and growing wise from learning something new, they are thrown into an identity crisis.

In the history of the church we see many divisions precipitated by unteachableness. The Bible does not say that if we all have an agreement of doctrine we will be unified. It does say that nothing can separate us from the love of Christ. Love, not knowledge, is what facilitates us to learn from one another. Through love we can share truth with one another and so grow up into Christ who is the omniscient One.

SPIRIT

This final category belongs to the spirit, the part of man through which he relates to the noumenal or unseen spirit world. Continue to mark personality blocks you identify with.

DELUSIONS

When deception becomes chronic, it may develop into delusion. A middle-aged woman, whose husband had once been unfaithful to her, had great difficulty forgiving him. At the slightest whim or fancy, she kept seeing her husband having affairs with other women. Although no evidence was ever established for any of her thoughts, their marriage almost crumbled under the strain. Without correction, delusion can develop to the paranoid, psychotic level where professional intervention becomes necessary.

RESENTMENT AND BITTERNESS

Resentment arises in our hearts when we fail to extend forgiveness. When hurt or wounded by a word, action or reaction, we face the choice to either forgive or resent. If we forgive, we are in the place to be forgiven by God for our own sins. But, if we allow resentment in our hearts, we also place a block in the way of God's forgiveness and open the door for bitterness to enter.

The Bible warns us to be careful lest there

spring up within any of us a bitter root through which many become defiled.[4] If we allow bitterness in our hearts, it's like a weed with a strong root planted within. Once we allow that root to be planted, soon it will spread to take over our heart and contaminate our mind, spirit and body.

In our garden in Hawaii we have sweated and toiled over a certain kind of weed that is a real menace. If the weed can be uprooted when it's just an inch or so in size, it's not bad, but if the root is left to get any bigger, we need a pick to destroy its long tap-like root.

Forgiving one another is what love is all about; not to forgive, is to become bitter and hard in spirit. Bitterness has destroyed many marriages, families and societies, and we don't want it to destroy us as well. Bitterness can also predispose us to both mental and physical disorders, which can only be successfully treated after forgiveness is first extended.

CRITICALNESS

A critical attitude leads to discontent, which then expels appreciation and gratitude. When this happens, our attention turns inward in the form of self-pity. We may try to present our penchant for pulling things apart as "positive criticism," but it's just the opposite because of its destructive root. Being hyper-critical is negative and can devastate others. We must learn to recognize the difference between "critical thinking," which sharpens us, and a "critical spirit" which cuts others down.

---

4. Hebrews 12:15

CONTROLLING AND POSSESSIVENESS

These two blocks in the wall around a person's heart are closely linked together, because one leads to the other. We may resort to control through insecurity and hurt, in an attempt to keep the upper hand. As we use control over and over, it develops into a possessive trait where we try to live another's life for them. This distortion becomes a lethal weapon in relationships, because it asphyxiates individuality.

MANIPULATION

We will now focus on perhaps the most powerful of all the blocks in our wall. Manipulation is a malignant and destructive aspect of personality holding the potential to simulate love yet block and destroy it. Because of this, manipulation is a major factor in marriage conflicts as well as in the disintegration of the family.

Manipulation can be defined as attempting to control people or circumstances through deceptive or indirect means. Webster's dictionary describes manipulation as insidious, meaning:

treacherous: awaiting a chance to entrap.

seductive: harmful but enticing.

subtle: developing so gradually as to be well established before becoming apparent, having a gradual but cumulative effect.

Manipulation[5] by nature is *dishonest*, but love, by contrast, works on the basis of honesty. The manipulator is dishonest in that he lives by a series of tricks, maneuvers, acts and role playing, until

---

5. Everett L. Shostrom, Man the Manipulator, (Nashville:Abingdon Press), pp. 45-46,50-51

it's often hard to discern who the real person is. The manipulator continually plays games with life, but the loving person is free and comfortable with himself. He can be genuine, and open with others in all sincerity.

The second aspect of manipulation is being unaware of what is happening. The manipulator has *tunnel vision*, seeing only what he wants to see, hearing what he wants to hear. Even though the situation may have been described in black and white, in clear, concrete terms, the manipulator still may appear not to have heard a word of it. As the manipulator focuses on his own primary gain, his conscience may be greatly dulled.

By contrast, the loving person is able to have a diversity of interests and receive from a diversity of input from his surroundings. He is not locked into things, but rather is relaxed and able to be aware of nature, music, the arts and beauty in the world.

The third aspect of manipulation is *control*. The manipulator lives his life as if he is a chess player with the ultimate goal of checkmating his opponent. The manipulator must have control at all costs, and so is always concentrating on the game of life. By contrast, the loving person doesn't need to be in control, but enjoys freedom in expression, and can relax.

The fourth aspect of manipulation is *distrust*. In relationships, the manipulator experiences great difficulty trusting others, and stemming from this difficulty, trusting himself. The manipulator constantly considers how to keep the upper hand and control his relationships, while the loving person, by contrast, enjoys relationships as a result of his freedom to trust.

Sadly most marriages today, are manipulative in origin. A man marries a woman to receive love from her, or a woman marries a man to get love and security. Both are manipulative, and poor foundations for marriage.

WHAT IS LOVE?

What is love in the biblical definition? Love is developing a relationship to *give*. Manipulation develops a relationship to *get*. For God so loved the world that He got us? NO! For God so loved the world that He gave his Son.[6] Our concept of love has become so distorted that our motive for loving is to get - "I need to get a wife," or "I need to get a husband." But that is not the motivation God designed for marriage, nor does it follow God's divine plumbline of love. Love is so often distorted in society. The media bombards us with something called love that is actually nothing but lust.

KINDS OF MANIPULATORS

There are four different kinds of manipulators I want to consider.

1. The *active* manipulator. The goal of this person is to maintain control at all costs. He avoids facing any of his weaknesses and exalts his strengths, always wanting to be the top dog. In his relationships he comes across as the strong one, capitalizing on others where ever possible.

2. The *passive* manipulator is a little more difficult to discern because his expression of

---

6. John 3:16

manipulation is not so overt. His goal is not control, but rather, to keep from offending. He plays the role of the helpless, needy person, often utilizing the block of self-pity in an attempt to win by losing. By playing the underdog, he manipulates his love needs from that position. While the active manipulator gets his way by winning, the passive manipulator wins by losing.

One day I saw both positions clearly illustrated when my family and I visited some friends. We had taken along our dog Sheba, but we were surprised when, as we busily greeted our friends, we heard a deep-throated snarl behind us. Turning around, there stood Sheba, stiff-legged with head and tail up, her golden coat bristling with indignation. On the ground before her lay our friend's big black dog, a picture of submission - lying on his back, with feet up and his pink tongue lolling. It was over after only a few moments, and both dogs spent the rest of the day chasing one another and playing. Sheba had apparently established herself as top dog, and the other was the underdog - at least in this relationship.

3. The *competitive* person is the third kind of manipulator. A little more versatile, the competitive person can play the under dog and top dog as the occasion requires, just by changing his maneuvers. More skilled and professional in developing manipulation in his personality, his goal is to win from any position. Other people are his competitors.

4. The *indifferent* manipulator is distinguished from the others because he doesn't like top dogs and he doesn't like under dogs. In fact he does not like dogs at all and is quick to say he doesn't care about dog games. But when he says he does not care, he is actually manipulating himself in a subtle way, deceiving himself through not acknowledging

how he really feels. He does care, and what's going on is a concern to him - but by denying and suppressing these feelings, he has manipulated himself. All of this is done in the name of *love* and is a subtle and powerful tool to destroy relationships.

Manipulators never rest, as if playing a continuous game of chess, they undergo tensions and pressures in order to obtain their goal. What is it they are reaching out for but never really able to attain?

As we follow the human plumbline of rejection to its end, it becomes apparent that the ultimate act of self-rejection is SUICIDE. The rising incidence of this as a cause of death is alarming. If however, we rather use the human plumbline of rebellion as a reference point in life, we are more likely to end up with a charge of HOMICIDE. In this case, we have vented our wrath on another instead of ourselves.

THE ONLY OPTION

You may feel that the options of pursuing human plumblines of rejection or rebellion are limited. Is there another choice? Yes, there is the true, Divine Plumbline. But wait! You must first consider what is involved. If we accept the Divine Plumbline to escape suicide and homicide - we must instead embrace being CRUCIFIED. "What an option!" you say.

What does being crucified mean? In essence, if we are to follow God's divine plumbline, we must be willing to accept the cross of Christ. We must crucify the carnal and unclean desires of our flesh that throw us from one side to the other in reaction. We must be willing to daily clean out the old desires and follow the new in truth and love, allowing selfishness, self-centeredness, lust and greed to die on the cross so Christ can live in us. "He who finds his life shall lose it, and he who loses his life will find it."[7]

In the next chapter, we will see how the walls we build form personality profiles. We will examine how far reaching are the effects of these walls on the individual, family and society.

COME ASIDE

Now go back over the blocks you identified with in your own life. How did you build them into the walls of your heart? Can you trace their origin?

Ponder the extenuating circumstances that caused the blocks to emerge.

Does their influence still affect you?

---

7. Matthew 10:39

CHAPTER 7

DIFFERENT STROKES
FOR DIFFERENT FOLKS

Reviewing the blocks we build into our walls can be depressing, especially as we contemplate how long some of them have been around. The walls of course, are symbolic not only of our defense systems, but also of personality types that begin to emerge from platforms of rejection or rebellion. In this chapter we will look at four possible personality profiles and seek to understand how and why they are developed. These are not the only forms, but are common personalities among us.

In considering character development there are both inherited and acquired aspects to personality. The nature versus nurture debate shows that it's not always easy to establish the line between what is fixed and what is variable in personality. However,

COMPLIANT CHRISTIAN

FIGURE 13

the Scriptures do give us some guidelines. In this study we are looking at the acquired or changeable aspects referred to in Ephesians 4:13, where Paul tells us of the need to grow up into the completeness of personality in Christ.

THE "COMPLIANT" CHRISTIAN

With her plumbline of rejection as a reference, the compliant Christian reaches out toward significant authority figures to fill her needs. The following statements may help us to understand her better:

"I'll help you with anything you want."
"I'll serve you at any time."
"I'll be loyal to you."
"I'll always affirm you."
"I'll pray regularly and faithfully for you."

On the other hand she expects the authority figure to:

"Notice me!"
"Affirm me."
"Be nice to me."
"Listen to me."
"Care about me."
"Be around for me when I need you."
"Never let me down or reject me."

Compliant persons can be tremendous servers and assistants. Often one step ahead of their leader, they are efficient and effective, as well as sensitive and caring. Involvement in counseling or ministry related work appeals to them.

The expressions of the compliant Christian can be narrowed down to two main responses:

"I'll do anything you want!"
"Please love me."

The compliant personality can be a very great

"CAN'T DO IT" CHRISTIAN

FIGURE 14

danger, both to themselves and the people to which they relate. Their needs for affirmation and love must be met, even at the expense of principle and truth. They tend toward procrastination and man-pleasing. Stemming from an inordinate desire for affection and affirmation, immorality is often a snare to them. If an authority figure fails them, either truly or in their imagination, they will take a deep plunge into rejection or depression. The more this happens, the more they withdraw and their ability to trust in future relationships is diminished. Too many of our spiritual leaders have succumbed to the subtle snare of the compliant personality, either in themselves or another.

An archetype of the compliant personality is found in the first book of Samuel.[1] After victory in battle, Saul disregarded instructions God had given for the destruction of the Amalekites. Seeking approval and recognition from men, he built a monument in his honor at Carmel. Because Saul feared men and wanted their affirmation, he did not fear and obey God. This compliancy led to a complete loss of his kingdom through a gradual, sad decline of his leadership.

When the compliant personality receives too many setbacks, he may change hats with the next personality profile.

THE "CAN'T DO IT" PERSONALITY

"No one cares about me anymore!"
"No one bothers to tell me what's happening."
"Nobody has time to listen to me."
"Nobody visits me anymore."

---

1. 1 Samuel 15:24

"No one comes to pray for me when I'm down
or ill."

"No one likes me."

As we come alongside the "Can't do it" personality these are some of the phrases we are sure
to hear at one stage or another. The great struggle
for this person is to feel he is wanted or useful .
We may also hear him say:

"It's no use trying anymore."

"I've failed so many times."

"I know I'm a failure!"

"I'll never be able to do it."

"I'll always be like this."

"I can't go on anymore."

"I quit!"

"I give up."

"God, why don't you make everything O.K.?"

This negative profile is not an uncommon one
in today's society. The two major messages emerging include:

"Nobody loves me."

"I give up."

One day the door of the counseling clinic
opened and in shuffled a man apparently young,
yet so stooped and forlorn he could have been mistaken for much older. Scuffing across the carpet
with his head down, his eyes furtively darted
around the room.

In a barely audible voice, he strained to answer
yes or no to our questions, and although we tried to
help, nothing we said seemed to make any impact
on him. It was almost as though he was encased in
armor, impervious to our efforts to break through
his barriers. After an extended counseling session,
we began to feel he was without hope. For years
he had wrestled with an internal conflict, plagued

with guilt from indulging in lust. By the time he had sought help from us he was so withdrawn and depressed there seemed little we could do. His crisis had become chronic, and in order to survive the real world, the young man had escaped into a fantasy world in the form of a manic depressive psychosis. This dramatically illustrated for me the truth of God's word - "The wages of sin is death."[2]

Due to a childhood sickness, Susan had been slightly handicapped. As far back as she could remember she had been ridiculed by her peers. As a result, she continually tried to please her parents, teachers and peers, in order to receive the love and affirmation she needed. An attractive woman, Susan had married young and given birth to six children, one right after the other.

Soon the effort to please her husband and her family became a real struggle. Instead of the affirmation she longed for, criticism was heaped upon her. No matter what she did, it never satisfied her husband. The food was over-cooked or not cooked enough; clothes were not ironed properly, or not folded right; the house was never in order, and nothing she did met with his approval. Her husband just ignored all her efforts to please him.

Gradually, over the years, Susan started viewing more and more TV, leaving all the household chores for her husband. Because her desires to please had been rejected, she withdrew, exchanging her compliant hat for the coat of armor of the "can't do it" personality.

Another illustration of this personality is Moses. Born and raised in rejection, Moses finally

---

2. Romans 6:23

COMPETITIVE CHRISTIAN

FIGURE 15

fled for his life when rejected by his people. Forty years later when God called him to lead His people out of slavery, Moses gave the typical response of this personality: "I can't!"[3]

The reference point in life for the "can't do it" personality is a plumbline of rejection, just as it is for the "compliant" personality. But instead of reaching toward their authority figures, the "can't do it" turns away, refusing any help. Often, after receiving so much hurt and pain from authority figures, their trust in others progressively diminishes. Because they cannot face the thought of another wounding experience, they withdraw from everyone into their armor. The deeper the hurts they receive, the more impenetrable their armor becomes until they vow, "I'll never be hurt again!"

Moving now from the passive lines of rejection over to the more aggressive lines of rebellion, we will examine two more personality profiles. The first personality prototype is more aggressive in his approach to authority figures than his compliant counterpart.

THE "COMPETITIVE" PERSONALITY

No other personality profile relates more to this humanistic age and its performance for love and acceptance. The programming of the competitive personality is probably the most common in western cultures. Someone with a competitive personality can often be overheard saying:

"I can do it better than any of you."

"I know it all. Just ask me!"

"I'll show you just how it should be done."

---

3. Exodus 4:1,10,13

"I'm just the person you've been looking for."
"Don't waste time taking a vacation."
"Don't be emotional."
"Be strong, don't show your weaknesses."

On the other hand, this person is looking for some affirming feedback and may give some of the following communication either verbally or non-verbally:

"Notice how well I do my job."
"Notice my excellent gifts and skills."
"See how indispensable I am."
"Praise my work and also me."
"Tell me I'm perfect and you'll make my day!"
"Don't ever tell me I'm a failure."

The message he is giving is: "I'm perfect. You have no option but to love me." He has been subtly programmed from childhood, that to be loved and affirmed, he must not only constantly achieve, but continue to strive to do even better.

The "immature evangelist" typifies this profile. With a roar of super-human energy he bursts into town, insisting on five-star treatment: the best hotel, the finest restaurants, free access to the telephone and expecting the church to pick up the bill. He gives dynamic messages, stirring up frenzied faith, but when he leaves town and the dust begins to clear, the truth comes out. He's left behind him a trail of wounded workers smarting from the pain of misuse and manipulation. Such competitive personalities use people to perform projects. To them, people are dispensable, but projects are not. They may develop the typical pattern of an over-achiever who in between spurts of performance becomes depressed and vulnerable.

Imagine a marathon where one of the runners tries to sprint the whole race. At the end of each spurt, way ahead of the others, he falls exhausted to the ground. Rallying all his strength, he again repeats the process, until after several sprints his stamina begins to wane. Finally he is overtaken by the other runners, and instead of being first, he is now last. Exhaustion, despair and disappointment overcome him as he struggles to finish the race.

The competitive Christian, like the runner and immature evangelist, can become susceptible to mental or physical illness as a result of burn out. Often in the storms of this man's ministry, family collapse, or financial ruin, God has been trying to get his attention. Lassoing him as he rides the Gospel trail, God topples him to the ground and exclaims, "Would you mind if I had a word with you?" This is not to accuse God of causing illness, or adversity, but He certainly has used its impetus as His opportunity in many lives.

A biblical example of the competitive personality is Jacob.[4] Known as the "supplanter," Jacob cheats his brother, Esau, out of his birthright. He then deceives his aged father for the first born's blessing, and is compelled to flee for his life. The 20 years in Haran hold little joy for Jacob, who meets his manipulative match in his uncle Laban. Finally, after many years of performing and competing, Jacob comes to the end of himself. During the trip to meet his brother Esau, Jacob's lifetime struggle against God culminates in a wrestling match with the angel of the Lord. By the end, Jacob is outwardly crippled, but inwardly renewed. Once a performer and manipulator, Jacob has become "Israel," which means "prince with God."

---

4. Genesis 27-30

CRITICAL CHRISTIAN

FIGURE 16

Bill was raised by parents who only gave their love and affirmation when he performed well in school or on the football field. After becoming a Christian, Bill's deep-seated parental program was transferred to his relationship with God. Becoming a pastor and a workaholic for God, Bill's health and family suffered as he continually performed for God's love and affirmation. In the trough of one of his frequent depressions, Bill fell into immorality with a compliant worker who hoped to fill her own need for love by pleasing him. Some of the characteristics of people with a competitive personality include the following:

They learned as children to perform.
They received affirmation only for doing well.
They have a real fear of failure.
They want compliments, but can't receive them.
Their center of worth is what others think of them.
They struggle to accept that they are lovable.
They can't take criticism.
They are defensive.
It is hard for them to be spontaneous.
They need to know the rules.
They can't receive a gift without giving one back.
They are continually striving to do something.
It is a great struggle for them to know how to live without performing.
It is a great struggle for them to sustain any intimate relationships.

THE CRITICAL CHRISTIAN

Another personality profile emerges around the

human plumbline of rebellion, where the person moves away from the authority figure in a more aggressive manner. You may hear them say:

"See how perfectly I perform."

"I'll show you just how it should be done."

"I know I am right!"

"Just listen to me!"

"I'm in charge."

On the other hand, the critical personality may make some harsh, condemning statements, such as the following:

"You'll never be any different."

"You're a hopeless case, that's what you are!"

"You're as stupid as the statement that you just made!"

"Can't you do it right?"

"You always mess up, don't you."

"It's all your fault."

The message they are giving is, "I'm unlovable and so are you!" The critical personality can most easily be seen in the example of an immature prophet. Every Sunday she comes to church with a quiver full of arrows and her bow held in readiness. She shoots her arrows into the congregation with great accuracy and effectiveness during the service, seeing her role as keeping everybody towing the line, including the pastor. He, on the other hand, is kept busy during the week, pulling out the arrows and dressing the wounds of his flock. He may also need some attention himself, especially if his sermons are not up to par! Of course, she gets a lot of feedback, but considers the persecution as part of her calling, only confirming that her arrows are hitting the mark!

Underneath this personality exterior are some very challenging presuppositions. First, she has lost faith in love. After being hurt in so many relationships, she has given up on love, concluding that she is unlovable. Instead of handling this hurt by passively withdrawing into some armor like the "can't do it" Christian, she has reacted aggressively, attacking others to convince them they, too, are unlovable. She firmly believes that others should fellowship with her in her suffering!

John's mother raised her son just as she had been raised, giving correction in the form of rejection. John learned what was wrong when he suffered alienation from his mother's love through doing something that displeased her. As a result, he developed a poor self-image and began a lifetime struggle with inferiority. Disciplining by rejection leaves a child suffering emotionally. The rejection communicated by the parent destroys a child's sense of worth, causing him to lose all motivation in life. Discipline and love must always go together. If this had happened in John's case he would not have suffered hurt from punishment.

Judas,[5] the betrayer of Jesus, is the perfect portrayal of a critical personality. In becoming negative and critical of Jesus and the disciples, he condemned not only the woman who anointed Jesus' feet with ointment, but blamed Jesus for allowing it to be wasted. In Judas' case, his critical spirit eventually led him to betray the Son of God. His bitterness and self-hatred finally brought him to end his own life in suicide.

CONCLUSION

In reviewing the four personality profiles we have examined, it is helpful to relate them to the four forms of manipulation discussed in chapter 5:

---

5. John 12:4

1. The *compliant* personality relates to the *passive manipulator*.
2. The *can't do it* personality relates to the *indifferent manipulator*.
3. The *competitive* personality relates to the *competitive manipulator*.
4. The *critical* personality relates to the *active manipulator*.

In considering what your own profile may be, it's helpful to recognize that we are not limited to only one! I initially developed a very compliant personality and later evolved more competitive traits to cope with my particular love deficit. It has been helpful for me to see my epistemology and to realize God's isn't finished with me yet!

These four profiles reflect on-going tension. Life in these categories is often impaired by one of the many stress disorders that not only debilitate people, but may also destroy them. Such disorders range from a great variety of skin diseases to severe strokes and fatal heart attacks. Many physical conditions may be warnings, signaling deeper maladies that lie within the personality structure.

Up to now, we have been looking at the walls of our hearts and the blocks we use to construct them. In this chapter we have also met four familiar personalities who have become good wall builders! Now we will go on to peep behind the wall itself to see one of the most insidious and malignant developments rearing its ugly head, both in the church and in the world today.

COME ASIDE

With which personality profiles do you identify?
Trace their origin and development in your life.

compliant   critical
competitive

Ponder those areas of weakness in your character
and formulate a strategy to change.

Visualize what you could do when you exchange
your weakness for strengths.

*Because authority figures failed me, I withdrew
+ the ability to trust in relationships
diminished.*

*Weaknesses — afraid of letting go,
fear of failure or failing someone
I try to be helpful — too much of a pleaser,
need for approval.*

CHAPTER 8

BEHIND OUR WALLS

"According to statistics, more people today die from over-eating than from starvation. In fact, most people dig their own graves with their teeth!" These words, spoken by one of my medical school professors as he began his lecture on obesity, have left a lasting imprint on my memory. During my years of medical practice, both in the developing and developed worlds, I have often pondered these words and found myself nodding in agreement.

Lust in both its overt and hidden forms, has resulted in great damage ever since man's inception. The serpent began with Eve and the forbidden fruit, and since then, that scene has been re-enacted over and over down through the centuries. Now let's peep through a hole in the wall to see how the Israelite leaders continued this "tradition:"

Kicking loose pebbles lying beside the temple walls, the prophet scuffed his way across the courtyard. Tiny clouds of dust rose behind each step. In the distance a dog barked, disturbing, momentarily, the heavy, almost ominous silence clinging to the massive stone blocks of the temple. Raising his bowed head, the prophet scrutinized the wall before him. Something seemed different. Was the wall beginning to crumble, or had a block been removed? Quickening his steps, the prophet found himself looking at a hole in the wall. Curious, he pressed his face against the sun-warmed rock and peered through the hole. Instantly he recoiled from the sight as shock waves rippled through his body. What sight paled his bronzed features? The prophet Ezekiel tells us that hidden behind those walls, Israel's leaders were having an idolatrous orgy.[1] Worshipping an image of the Canaanite goddess Asherah, they had totally departed from the true religion of Israel as they indulged in rebellious acts of lust.

The most insightful overview of such lust is found in 1 John 2:15-16. Here the lust of the flesh and the lust of the eyes are described as self-destructive indulgences. The lust of the eyes refers to an inordinate desire that has entered the mind through the eyegate. As the lust of the eyes relates to temptation, the lust of the flesh refers to actually yielding to that desire, finally coming under its evil influence and control.

LUST

How is it that so many of us become ensnared and then enslaved by lustful habits that detract from and even destroy our health and lives? Let's return with Ezekiel to peek behind the walls of

---

1. Ezekiel 8:6-12

man's heart, the walls behind which we practice our secret sins and idolatry.

We build these walls of defense to protect us from enemies who wound us. These enemies, real or imagined, strongly influence our responses to life. But what happens behind our walls? How do we get enslaved by lustful habits? Let's look at an illustration to help answer these questions.

In Figure 17, the line marked "A" represents the plumbline of rejection by a significant authority figure, hanging like a tilted plumbline throwing everything in the person's life askew. The most immediate emotion the person will have to handle when he experiences this rejection is hurt or inner pain. Seeing this kind of pain in my patients eventually became a greater challenge to me than the physical pain I saw so much of in my general medical practice. Many more patients suffered with emotional pain than physical pain, yet there seemed so little I could do to alleviate this inner suffering. In search of answers I began asking some questions of my patients that were in obvious emotional pain. I learned many women especially, have a well-worn path to the refrigerator or cookie jar. Soon similar patterns began to emerge and a whole new dimension of understanding opened up to me. Each time I asked how they coped with their inner pain, their answers sounded something like this:

"I eat more."
"I drink more."
"I go on a spending spree."
"I take drugs."
"I go out and have an affair."
"I get drunk."

FLIGHT SWING

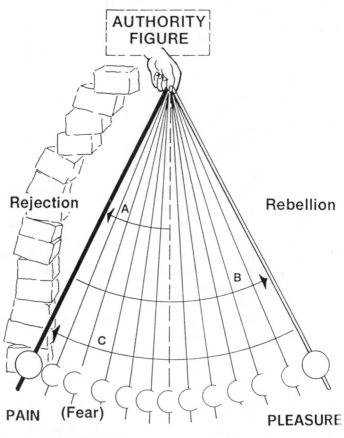

AUTHORITY
FIGURE

Rejection

Rebellion

A

B

C

PAIN   (Fear)

PLEASURE

A. REJECTION BY   B. FLIGHT
   AUTHORITY FIGURE   C. RETURN

FIGURE 17

In each case, my patients were trying to flee for relief from pain into some kind of pleasure. I call this the FLIGHT SWING as labeled in Figure 17. What my patients were not accepting was that the pleasure was only temporary, and they would later be swinging back to the pain to begin the same cycle over again. In Figure 17, the line labeled "B" represents the swing away from pain toward pleasure, and "C" is the eventual return to the pain and the beginning of another cycle.

This process was made very clear to me one day when a middle-aged woman came to my office for help. Mrs. Beasley's first words were to inform me of her overweight problem, and after a quick glance I didn't need any convincing. When she continued straight on to request a prescription to magically transform her figure, I explained she needed to tell me about herself and her family.

I soon discovered her husband was an alcoholic whose lifestyle gave her much grief and shame. Obviously, both this woman and her husband had experienced great pain in their lives and the only difference between them was their choice of pleasures used to ease the pain.

Now their chosen pleasures were turning into additional pain as Mrs. Beasley grew more and more obese, Mr. Beasley became ill from alcohol, and the whole family sunk deeper into poverty. Here we see exemplified what John spoke about, namely the lust of the flesh and the lust of the eyes.

ANOREXIA NERVOSA

Another condition illustrating the Flight Swing is Anorexia Nervosa, a medical malady especially found in young women who, out of an emotional trama may starve themselves to the point of malnutrition and even death. A majority of these cases are the daughters of wealthy, success-oriented parents who place great demands on their children, often beyond their capabilities. When the parents withhold love until expectations are met, the young women frequently experience a frantic striving to achieve, motivated by underlying guilt and remorse for failing to live up to these expectations. Left with a chronic, inner feeling of emptiness and pain, they then flee to the pleasure found in eating. When the temporary pleasure ends, they are seized by a fear of fatness and more rejection. Usually they then find a private place and induce vomiting, or perhaps turn to laxatives to purge themselves of the calories. In an attempt to escape criticism, the young women adopt a lifestyle of deceptiveness, secretive eating, vomiting and denial. Sadly, about 20% of these girls die from malnutrition and its complications. Another 20% have great difficulty breaking out of a cycle of swinging from pain to pleasure based on an inner lust for approval.

APPETITES OUT OF CONTROL

In my own case, I developed an addictive use of two forms of pleasure during childhood as a result of the pain of my teacher's ridicule.

The first was eating. Food became like a fix. If I didn't have food at the right time I was a bundle of nerves, and when I did get it I gulped it down like an animal.

The other false comfort I used as an analgesic was my fantasy world. Using some of the stories of filth and lust shared around the school grounds, I developed my own private, fantasy smut library seeking some relief. As always, the pleasure was short-lived and I soon developed a garbage can mentality. Later, after becoming a Christian, these two areas of addiction became my great battle ground. I later learned that food and sex are two common escapes, and are often related.

Just as we have appetites for food or alchohol, we also have an appetite for sex. Promiscuity, immorality and homosexuality are rampant today, even in spite of the AIDS threat. Because lust has become so widespread, many couples fail to learn the meaning of true love in its highest form.

The Bible shows us that lust demands and imposes itself on another, while love sacrifices itself for the needs of another. Lust *gets* at any price, while love *gives* at any price. Often the cruder, short term drive to fulfill lust overrides the more sensitive, long term goal for relationship.

Drugs, whether prescribed or bought illegally, have become a multi-billion dollar business. Many today live in the stupor of prescribed or self-induced addiction. Teenagers are throwing away their youth and their lives into bio-chemical lust traps, trying to escape the emotional pain they can't bear to face.

PLEASURE AND PAIN

Dr. Richard Solomon, professor of psychology at the University of Pennsylvania undertook research for the National Institute of Mental Health on "The Costs of Pleasure and the Benefits of Pain." He explains how an unconditional stimulus most often results in three major phenomena:

A pleasurable experience,

An addictive pattern, and

A painful withdrawal.

His theory is called "The Opponent-Process Theory of Acquired Motivation." This theory gives a plausible account of addictive behaviors, initiated by either painful or pleasurable events. His experi-

FIGHT SWING

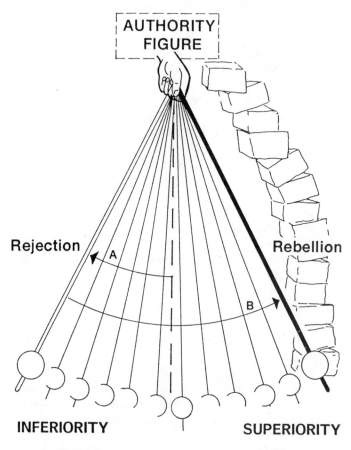

FIGURE 18

mentation included work with drug addictions, social attachments, sensory cravings and aversive stimuli.[2] Among the conclusions he draws are:

1. When addiction to a pleasure sets in, it is usually offset by an opposing pain.

2. This opponent pain is sluggish both in its development and its relief.

3. The opponent process is strengthened by use at appropriate time intervals.

4. Repeated pleasures lose much of their pleasantness and make one potentially capable of new sources of suffering.

For example, the overeater wrestles with some of the ailments of obesity. The sexually indulgent contracts a venereal disease.

Solomon's research adds weight to the pleasure/pain already discussed. The more addictive we become, the more suffering we open ourselves to. Solomon concedes to his theory having a puritan moral aspect. He could be referring to the biblical truth of using self control in all things.[3]

Many counselors facilitate repentance over the sinful pleasure in their clients, but fail to deal with the residual pain. But then, without relief from the analgesic, the individual is left in more intensive pain, and either falls into a relapse of the old pleasure, or begins to substitute with another. This explains, to some extent, why many so easily fall back into old patterns.

How then are we to deal with this pain, if not through pleasure? The answer lies hidden in the pages ahead.

---

2. Richard L. Solomon, "The Opponent-Process Theory of Acquired Motivation," American Psychologist, Aug. 1980, pp.691-712
3. 1 Corinthians 9:25

THE PRIDE OF LIFE

In 1 John 2:15-16, a second element called the pride of life is described as being of the world and therefore not of the Father. Back in the garden of Eden, the devil used the partnership of lust and pride to make a touchdown for sin in the game of life. Adam and Eve proved to be no match against the cunning and deceptive moves of lust and pride, and ever since man has suffered in their hands. The slain of pride and lust are strewn down the playing fields of history, just as scripture says, "Pride comes before a fall ..."[4]

As we look at Figure 18, we see that swing "A" once again represents the result of rejection by an authority figure. Now, instead of the emotions being a battleground, the mind faces the onslaught as thoughts of inferiority flood over it. At one time or another most of us wrestle with such thoughts, but we react in different ways. The more passive believe and accept feelings of inferiority, doing the best they can under the circumstances. But the aggressive person rises up and endeavors to prove not only that he's not inferior, but that he's actually superior, as is reflected in swing "B" in Figure 18.

This dynamic is illustrated in one of the most powerful philosophical movements of our day, atheistic/secular humanism. Rejecting God in an extreme expression of pride, the secular humanist attempts to replace God with his own self. But he still faces gross limitations within himself, so he tries to compensate for those limitations by moving into the superiority swing in an attempt at proving his own deity. Simple pleas for more humane

---

4. Proverbs 16:18

treatment are heralded by this philosophy at first, but soon frustrations arise in what becomes, if taken to its extreme, a "superman philosophy." Man has become a product which must be perfected at any cost, so he is then only of value if he functions perfectly. With this line of thought, euthanasia, selective abortion, and sperm banks are all logical methods of eliminating the handicapped and propagating a superior species.

Because secular humanism so permeates our western society, many have fallen by the wayside from broken marriages, broken families and poor health. The fallout due to this philosophy is phenomenal!

BROKEN PEOPLE

One example of a group which rebelled against such a philosophy are the hippies of the 60's. Swinging toward what they believed was a superior lifestyle for the welfare of human beings, they took special consideration for individuality and humanity. Unfortunately the movement degenerated into license for abusing drugs, immorality and food fads. Many young people who swung toward freedom, ended only in another, deeper bondage. Let me share an example of such a couple.

The first time I met Peter and Trish, they were living together in a tree house. Trish, draped in a loose fitting dress, was pregnant with her first child. Peter, long haired and bearded, also wore a long, flowing gown streaked with grime and dirt. A strong, unpleasant odor emanated from him. Not long after that first encounter, Peter came to see me at the counseling clinic. In the confines of my dimly lit office, he sat cross-legged on the floor with the folds of his flowing gown drawn up between his legs. A dirty cloth bag lay on the carpet beside him, and his eyes had a glazed, slightly drugged appearance. Throughout the hour long session, Peter kept reaching into his bag to get out tiny mushrooms which he then munched noisily. Later I learned he was eating what the hippies called "magic mushrooms." Grown in cow dung, these mushrooms were so potent that they rendered a hallucingenic effect similar to LSD. No wonder his eyes were glazed and we had so much trouble communicating!

As I asked question after question, Peter only seemed to answer "philosophically." The smell in the room was so bad that when Barbara joined me in the session she felt nauseous and had to keep her hanky jammed against her nose. She later confessed she didn't understand a word Peter said, as if he were on another planet. It's no wonder we got nowhere that day. But over the months Barbara drew close to Trish and it was from her that we learned his story.

Peter was 20, married, and in the air force when he was sent to the island of Guam. His job was to plot the weather for the B-52 bombers, as well as briefing pilots for the weather they would face on Viet Nam bombing missions. Peter had been against the war from the beginning so when his marriage broke up and no family ties held him back, he rejected the air force completely. He then began the long, hard, hippy trail that led him through South East Asia and finally to Hawaii. Immersed in Eastern philosphies and continually high on drugs, Peter wasted some of the best years of his life just wandering up and down the island of Hawaii. When he met Trish, a lonely, lost girl, he invited her to be part of his life. But by the time we met them, both were coming to the end of their rope and their life of no restraint.

Remarkably, God became the Rescuer who turned this couple from their dead-end life style and philosophies. Today they are a happily married couple, and a changed Peter went back to college to be the effective school teacher he is today. This couple's story could be told repeatedly by many disillusioned young people who threw away all the old traditions in reaction to society, only to find the new and sometimes devastating ones allowed them to subtly drift into such lustful philosophies and lifestyles.

BEING "THE BEST" AT ANY COST

Not all, however, swing into overt rebellion. Some choose to fight lustily to be *"The Best"* at something. Many dreamed for decades to be one of the first astronauts on the moon. A tremendous goal, it would take much training, competing, striving and performing.

One man who was willing to pay the price with a view to eliminating his inferiority actually became such an astronaut. At first revelling in his glory, he then realized the honor was a short-lived run at fame and affirmation. Other astronauts soon followed his path, and not only did he begin losing his fame, he also lost the boost the accomplishment had given his self image. The moon walk hadn't met his love deficit, and his old struggles became worse. When his feelings of inferiority returned, he started drinking to cover the pain, and so began

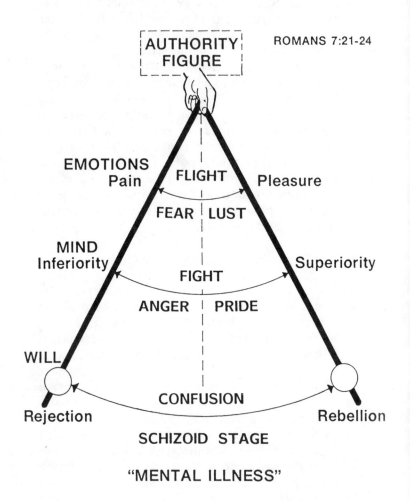

FIGURE 19

the downhill slide into alcoholism.

The examples are endless of those who seemingly won their way to the top, only to find their love deficits deepened by loneliness. The pride of life is what I call a FIGHT swing, where an individual unrelentingly strives, competes and performs to establish his superiority and therefore his acceptability, among the human race. In this philosophy, failure is not a consideration and the end justifies the means.

Figure 19 takes us another step in this "soul swing." Here we see both lust and fear are catalysts for an emotional swing, fleeing from pain into pleasure. We have already discussed how inner pain can be alleviated by pleasure, which, as compulsive or addictive patterns develop, becomes lust. Fear may also develop, such as the fear of being left without our pleasure, the fear of becoming a slave to that pleasure, or both, as in alcoholism.

On the other hand, pride and anger can be catalysts for a mind swing. For example, a man trying to climb the corporate ladder may have an inner, hidden agenda of trying to prove he is not inferior, but actually superior to others, manifesting his pride. When he is one day suddenly fired, that pride is deeply hurt, and he swings over to thoughts of anger. Although he may appear to be controlled at first, his inner hostility is openly expressed to his family once he goes home. In the same way, when any of us swing toward superiority out of pride, we later will swing toward inferiority when that pride is hurt through some failing. Uncontrolled anger and hostility may also be expressed often devastating our loved ones.

After this, the third part of the soul, called the will, is greatly weakened. As the will continues to

THE FINAL SWING

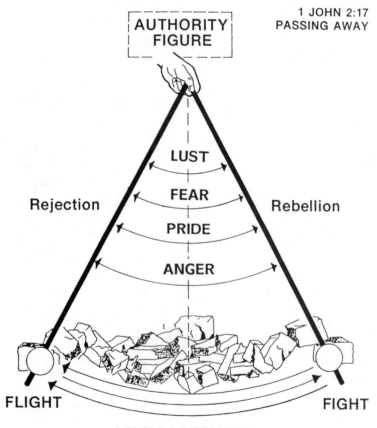

1 JOHN 2:17
PASSING AWAY

AUTHORITY FIGURE

LUST

FEAR

PRIDE

ANGER

Rejection

Rebellion

FLIGHT

FIGHT

DOUBLE-MINDEDNESS
JAMES 1:7,8

FIGURE 20

be manipulated by the mind and the emotions, confusion sets in. Both tension and exhaustion build up to the point of instability, causing breakdown in one form or another, as is depicted in Figure 20.

In each of these soul swings, whether through the emotions, mind or will, we will see lust, fear, pride, anger and other ingredients undermine the walls of the personality until they fall down, either in part or as a whole. When we go beyond the limit of pressure and tension we can endure, we will enter the breakdown zone. Walls we have built may then come tumbling down in a collapse of control over our lives, meaning the body, mind, and spirit functions.

James' epistle [5] refers to "double-mindedness," which in the original Greek is better translated "double-souled." This means there is a "double soul set" or a "double set" of mind, will and emotions. We might say the individual has two mind-sets, at war with each other. Figure 20 depicts this with rejection as one mind set and rebellion as the other. If we swing between them, we become increasingly unstable and heighten our potential for breakdown. Mental and emotional health then becomes precarious.

The context of the word "double-minded" in the book of James refers to causes of unbelief, stating that a double-minded man is "unstable in all of his ways." The word "all" here infers that mental illness or breakdown may result from soul swings brought on by lust, fear, pride and anger. Then we will begin to swing back and forth in a wildly inconsistent manner, as shown in Figure 20.

God has another way for these walls of re-

---

5. James 1:6-8

jection and rebellion to come down in a much more constructive and healing manner. As we go on to look at God's dealings with His own people Israel, we will see how, when our old walls come down, the Lord will build new walls in our lives.

COME ASIDE

Recall some of the painful experiences of your life.

Describe how you handled the inner pain and give the results. *withdraw seek to excel in areas or pursue college or excellence of some kind*

How have you handled increasing stress in your life? *pray, walk, cry, sometimes a small amount to drink*

CHAPTER 9

REBUILDING THE FOUNDATIONS

"And the high fortifications of your walls [the Lord] will bring down, lay low, and bring to the ground, even to the dust."[1]

"In that day shall this song be sung in the land of Judah: We have a strong city; [the Lord] sets up salvation as walls and bulwarks."[2]

The above references are an excellent summary of how we build walls in our lives, but with a new theme than has been previously discussed. The Lord says in these passages it is not His desire to leave us defenseless and vulnerable to all that the enemy of our souls would hurl at us. Instead, He desires to give us a new wall called salvation[3] with gates called praise, to protect us from destruction and devastation.

---

1. Isaiah 25:12, Amplified Bible
2. Isaiah 26:1, Amplified Bible
3. Isaiah 60:18, Amplified Bible

THE MINOR PROPHETS

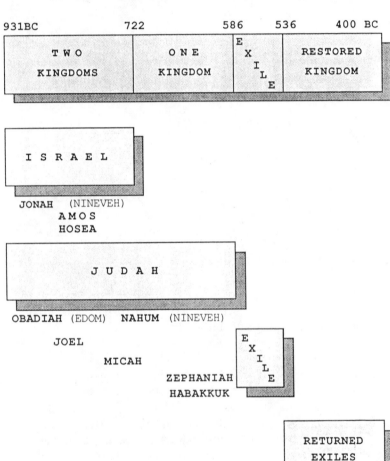

FIGURE 21

In this next part of our study, we will look at how, after the walls of rejection and rebellion have been brought down and the rubble removed, the walls of salvation can be built into our lives.

To see how God deals in our lives, let's review some of Israel's history, starting when its kingdom was divided. The chart as illustrated in Figure 21 gives us a brief overview of the events.

Failing to heed anointed warnings by Amos and Hosea, Israel went into exile. Although the nation of Judah saw what had happened and were likewise warned by a powerful prophetic team, they also failed to repent. As a consequence, both Israel and Judah suffered many years in servitude to Babylon.

During these years of Jewish exile, historic changes took place. First, the power of Babylon crumpled and perished before the resistless spread of the Persian empire. Then the cry of God's chosen, but sorely chastened people, reached Him from among the exiles. He responded to their cry by raising up leaders to guide His people back into the land of their inheritance.

The first remarkable leader was a Gentile king named Cyrus, who felt God's stirring to put a proclamation in writing: A temple would be built in Jerusalem for the Lord and people were needed for the task. Cyrus gave back the stolen temple treasures to facilitate the move, and as a result, 42,360 Israelites returned to Jerusalem under the leadership of Zerubbabel and several others. Let's follow the development of possibly the most significant people group movement the world has ever seen.

Imagine how this group of dusty, travel-worn people felt as they returned from exile, only to find

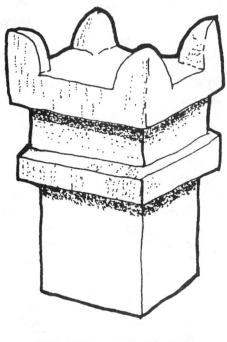

THE ALTAR

FIGURE 22

their inheritance reduced to a pile of rubble and ruins. Ezra 3:1-6 tells how all the returning exiles gathered together as one man for the first significant event in Jerusalem - the building of the Altar.

Before there could be worship, a sacrifice had to be made for the sins of the people, showing how worship is only acceptable to God when sin is being dealt with. The altar is the place where we come and enter into reconciliation with God, where we begin to take responsibility for sin, and where we begin to partake of our redemption. The altar with its various offerings, and especially with its freewill offerings, symbolically speaks of consecration to God. The new altar was built in Jerusalem just where the former one had been, representing how the old-time worship was re-established and restored. The exiles recognized that if they were going to be successful in rebuilding the temple, they needed the blessing, strength and grace of Jehovah. But not just for the exiles, but for us as well, we see the altar has great significance. It is a place of:

CONFESSION
SACRIFICE
REPENTANCE
FORGIVENESS
ATONEMENT
ACCEPTANCE
DELIVERANCE
HEALING
PROTECTION
BLOOD.

When we first receive Christ as our savior, we come to the altar - but this does not mean that we

THE TEMPLE

FIGURE 23

never sin again. All too often when we do sin, we fail to go back to the altar. As a result, "little sins" build up in our lives, and if left unconfessed, they bring a separation between us and God. Soon we find it difficult to hear God's voice, and our love for Him begins to wane.

Israel learned this the hard way, as many of us do today. Our altar can become so overgrown it gets lost among the weeds, and only with the use of a machete can we find it again. In any revival people must first repent, confess their sins and return to the altar to be restored to full fellowship with God.

We all need to follow that well-worn path to the altar as often as we sin. We are called to be holy as He is holy,[4] and the scriptures say that without holiness, no man shall see the Lord.[5]

Next, under the leadership of Zerubbabel the priest, the children of Israel built the temple of the Lord, described in Ezra 3:7-13. The temple is the place where God is worshipped, where we have fellowship with Him and one another. Just as we need to have an altar established in our hearts, so we need a temple, or a place that belongs exclusively to the Lord. We need a place where we put aside all else and go into His presence to worship and be still before Him. Here is where we will be refreshed and restored, and our relationship with Him will be deepened. As in those days, the temple has great significance in our lives. It is a place of:

WORSHIP
THANKSGIVING
FELLOWSHIP

---

4. 1 Peter 1:15
5. Hebrews 12:14

GIVING
PRAYER
WITNESS
SACRAMENT
THE PRESENCE OF GOD
JOY
HOLINESS
POWER
ANOINTING.

In each of these aspects, we see how the temple was the place where God's presence dwelt. At times, those who ministered in the temple were unable to stand on their feet because the presence of the Lord was so overwhelming, something we only hope to glimpse today. But the moment the foundation of the temple was finished, the Israelites went wild in celebration. Ezra 3:11 lists how some shouted, some sang, and others wept, all so loudly that the noise could be heard far away.

Why were they so deeply moved? They knew the temple meant God's presence would be amongst them once again. The exiles who had been in the temple during King Solomon's day wept from the deep longing to see God's presence return among them again in power and grace.

What is the state of your personal temple? Does it lie in ruins, badly needing restoration? Have you let it turn to shambles through neglect and the busyness of life? How important is it for you to have God's presence filling your temple day by day? So often we are so busy in our work for the Lord, that we don't have time for Him. We must see that the work of our hands is only acceptable to Him as an overflow of our love relationship with the Lord. That relationship is developed, nourished, strengthened and established in the temple, yet so often we push it to the side when pressures, demands, and even legitimate, good things crowd our day.

Several years ago, I was conducting a seminar in Penang, Maylasia, when God brought me to a place of accountability, challenging me to face these questions. Penang, called the "Pearl of the Orient" and a "city of a thousand temples," has long been a stronghold of idolatry. Proselytizing is illegal in Maylasia, so we had to get special permission for me to speak to the several hundred people in the seminar. One hot, steamy night, near the end of the week-long ministry, I invited people up for prayer.

Malaysia is a country where an exotic blend of the Malay, Chinese and Indian cultures meet. On this night, as I stood before the people gathering before me, their striking beauty was reflected in the diversity of their attire. But their beauty did nothing to appease the emptiness I was feeling deep within. Seeing a beautiful Indian woman weeping, I began to pray for her but found myself with little feeling, unable to identify. She confided she was a divorcee, crushed with the pain and hurt of the separation, and although I was aware of God working in her life, I somehow felt detached and even distant.

Later, back in my plush hotel room, I sensed that while it had been a powerful night, something had been wrong. While I had watched the Holy Spirit set others free, why had I remained cold and apart? Kneeling beside the bed, I asked the Lord for the answer to my hardness and indifference. It was almost midnight by then, and I felt tired and drawn from the week's ministry. Still I pushed myself to pray.

THE WALL OF SALVATION

EZRA = RECONCILIATION

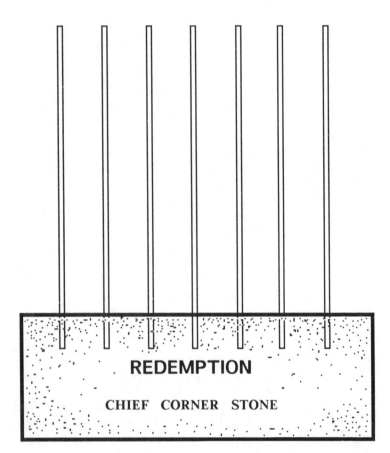

FIGURE 24

At last I heard Him say, "Bruce, you've been so busy with my work, that you haven't had time for me." All at once I saw how the past few months had been filled with seminars, appointments and ministry, to the point that I neglected the altar of intimacy with Him. I had made an idol of my ministry and had worshipped at its shrine instead of at the Lord's feet. I clearly saw how the grace of God had continued to bless His word through me, but because of my neglect, I had remained on the outside looking in.

With tears of repentance, I humbled myself and found grace to return to the temple in my heart, waiting for the enriching refreshment of His presence and His joy.

Since then I have seen how many of us do not require the Lord's presence as our vital need. In the Psalms,[6] David speaks of how happy, fortunate and to be envied are those who dwell in the house and presence of the Lord. They experience His joy, comfort and strength, as well as every good thing needed for His service. To neglect the temple, or the place of intimacy with God, is to become vulnerable to worshipping other "gods," falling into error and becoming lost in an idolatrous maze of religion. Only by being in His presence will our being begin to reflect His.

Just as in Ezra's day, we need to first return to the altar in repentance and then take care not to neglect His temple. Since the days of the early church, we can take these first two steps because of Christ's atoning work on the cross. Christ is called the Chief Cornerstone in 1 Peter 2:4-8, and that Chief Cornerstone must become both the altar and the temple of our lives in an ongoing basis. Until

---

6. Psalm 84:5-12

we put the Lord in His proper place in our lives, salvation cannot be experienced nor any progress made. Putting this all together as we view Figure 24, we see that the foundation for the wall of our salvation is the stone of **REDEMPTION**:

> ... *says the Lord God, Behold, I am laying in Zion for a foundation a Stone, a tested Stone, a precious Cornerstone of sure foundation; he who believes (trusts in, relies on, and adheres to that Stone) will not be ashamed or give way or hasten away (in sudden panic). I will make justice the measuring line and righteousness the plummet; and hail will sweep away the refuge of lies, and waters will overwhelm the hiding place (the shelter).*[7]

These verses draw the picture of a storm sweeping away the refuge of lies and walls of rejection and rebellion. Once gone, these walls are replaced with a tested and sure cornerstone upon which the walls of salvation can be built. Now these walls are built evenly and securely, in line with righteousness - measured by the DIVINE PLUMBLINE.

In the next chapter, we will see how we can build these walls as our own salvation.

---

7. Isaiah 28:16-17, Amplified Bible

COME ASIDE

Review the role and function of the altar in your life.

How can you grow in intimacy with God? Write your plan.

Consider the foundations of your faith.

CHAPTER 10

DISCOVERING FATHER

Now the rebuilt temple stood in Jerusalem, but only crumbled walls surrounded the holy city. For the task of rebuilding the city walls, God raised up Nehemiah to lead the third and last group of the Israelites to return home from Persia.

The name "Nehemiah" means "comforter and counselor, or consoler," symbolizing how the Holy Spirit comes alongside to guide and strengthen us in the ways of God. In the natural life, Nehemiah was a cupbearer, wall builder and governor, while in spiritual life, he challenges us to drink from the Lord's cup, build up the walls of salvation, and prepare ourselves to rule and reign with Jesus.

The book of Ezra we studied in chapter nine is a book of reconciliation, while the book of Nehemiah centers on the restoration of Israel to her God-given inheritance.

As cupbearer to the Persian King in the winter palace at Susa, Nehemiah heard some discouraging reports about his homeland: Jerusalem's defenses were left in ruins, and the people were continually harassed. Although far away, Nehemiah was so concerned for his people that for four months he continued to mourn and intercede for the situation.

It is appropriate to ask, "What is our response when God delivers a message to us through one of His couriers?" Do we, like Nehemiah, receive that word seriously? All too often, I believe we don't recognize He is speaking to us, or worse, we forget what He said just a few days later. In the book of Nehemiah, we read how he poured out his heart to God for one, two, three, and even four months before he received an answer. In verse 5 of the first chapter we see that as Nehemiah waited before the Lord, he began praising God for keeping His covenant and for being loving and kind to those who keep His commandments. How could Nehemiah, in the face of the destruction of his homeland, respond so positively in praise? Clearly, he must have received a revelation of God's nature and character, so that in the midst of seemingly hopeless circumstances he could respond with praises to God for His faithfulness.

KNOWING WHAT IS REAL

By praising God in the difficult situation, Nehemiah wasn't denying its reality, but he was linking it up to *the God who is reality,* the one greater than any challenge on earth. By worshipping and exalting God for who and what He is, Nehemiah brought the God of possibilities into an impossible situation.

Just as the scriptures tell us He inhabits the praises of His people, when we praise God He comes and dwells in our midst. As we begin to see Him and touch Him, our faith is quickened, and hope is released. Then the situation that once seemed so impossible is seen in the light of who God is, and it shrinks to the proper perspective.

As Nehemiah began to praise and worship the Lord, faith was lifted up in his heart to see God's people come in line with His plumbline and God's promises restored. Nehemiah could then say along with Job, "I have heard of you with the hearing of the ear, but now my (spiritual) eye sees you."[1]

What did Job mean? He had heard so much about God, and lived in the light of that truth, but when God allowed him to be tested, Job received a revelation of himself, and under deep conviction, repented in dust and ashes. "Now my spiritual eyes see YOU!" was his cry. Job was saying that in some new and exciting way he had come into a contact with Father God. He had come into the place where revelation poured into his heart and life, a place God desires to take all of us - but it often comes in the midst of difficult circumstances, just as Job and Nehemiah experienced. If we also respond with praise in our own wilderness experiences, we will also receive the revelation we need to pass the test.

In Figure 25, we see the foundation stone of *Redemption*, with Christ as the Chief Cornerstone. To give strength to the wall of salvation as it is built are seven iron reinforcing rods. As we've seen from Nehemiah's example, the first rod that rises from the foundation stone is the rod of *Revelation*.

Revelation is not just new knowledge or deeper understanding, but is insight that makes such an

---

1. Job 42:5

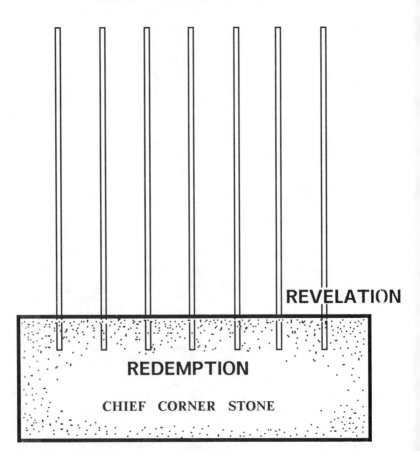

FIGURE 25

impact on the heart that a change of lifestyle results. Revelation is not received on the basis of IQ, but it is received by those who are obedient to God's word. A little child with an open heart may receive greater revelation than some professor of religion with several degrees! According to Psalm 119:97-100, those who are obedient may acquire more revelation than their teachers, elders and enemies. At the same time, disobedience leads to deception and a loss of revelation.

INTIMACY WITH THE FATHER

In the Gospel of John,[2] Jesus speaks to His disciples concerning His departure. They thought He was preparing to overthrow the tyrannical Roman rule and establish His own kingdom, so they were deeply perplexed by Jesus' words of an imminent departure. What would become of their political dreams? Thomas first broke the troubled silence by boldly telling Jesus the facts. Since they just learned He was going away, how could they know where He was going, or how to get there? Jesus cut through all their preconceived ideas with the words: "I am the Way, the Truth and the Life; no one comes to the Father but by Me."[3]

The disciples could only wonder. What did Jesus mean? Then He told them He was going to another place, not an earthly kingdom, but a heavenly one with the Father. Jesus was trying to tell the disciples not to stop on "the way" but to go all the way to their destination, which is intimacy with the Father. Jesus is the way to the Father,

2. John 14:1-6
3. John 14:6

whom we also need to go on to know. He doesn't want us to be saved only to be left as orphans, but the Father longs for intimacy with us.[4] He desires to come with Jesus and dwell in us, His temple, as Friend and Father. For the disciples, what had been knowledge before had now become revelation. What had before been confined to their intellects had now become part of their lives.

Why can it be so hard for us to follow Jesus to the Father? Why do many of us stay as orphans, when Jesus longs for us to join Him as the Father's son or daughter? Over and over as I've counseled people, I've seen fears, inhibitions, misgivings or other chains hinder us from going on to receive the Father's love. The following illustration will help us see why.

OBSTACLES

Lydia, while attending a YWAM school of discipleship, was quiet and attentive during the first few weeks. When an opportunity was given for students to share experiences before the class, Lydia was quick to respond.

"I come from a large family of eight children," Lydia's said in a soft but clear voice. Everyone grew quiet in the open pavilion, and only the birds squabbling in the coconut palms disturbed the stillness.

"When I was a teenager, my mother was diagnosed with terminal cancer," Lydia explained. "I had to drop out of school to start running the home, and I was really disappointed not to finish my studies or graduate with my friends. My mother died some months later, and because I was

---

4. John 14:21,23

the oldest, the task of caring for the rest of the children fell on my shoulders. I really struggled to understand why God let Mother die, but every day my father read the Bible and prayed with us, which really comforted me."

Lydia paused and glanced around the filled pavilion. "One evening, my father approached me and invited me to his room," she began again hesitantly. "He told me my new responsibilities also involved taking over for my mother as his mate." Shock waves rippled across the pavilion as Lydia brushed tears from her eyes and shared softly that an incestuous relationship then began with her father. When she later became pregnant, her father told her the child would become a brother or sister in the family.

Later during her pregnancy, Lydia talked with one of her younger sisters and learned she had also become sexually involved with their father. Both wanted to trust their father, yet wrestled with deep guilt feelings. The more they talked the worse they felt. The nine months of Lydia's pregnancy were overshadowed by guilt and shame, clouding out any joy and anticipation of motherhood.

"I began to resent my father," she continued. "Between periods of hostility toward him, I went up and down on a rollercoaster relationship of love and hate. A growing desire began to grip me to leave behind all the paradoxical pressures that had become so confusing and depressing." Lydia said that her father also sensed her conflict, so he tried to intimidate her with verbal threats and bribes. Her only relief was in the deep love she had for her newborn son Joey, who as he grew older, was told he was her younger brother.

Finally the day came when Lydia could handle

it no longer. Bundling up a few belongings, she gathered the small store of money she had secretly laid aside for this inevitable occasion. Battling between the guilt of leaving and the horror of staying another day, questions ran over and over through Lydia's mind. Her family had suffered so much grief when their mother died, and now the only other "mother" they knew was suddenly disappearing from their lives with their youngest "brother."

"How could I do it? Yet on the other hand, how could I not do it!" Lydia wept before us, experiencing the pain again. Deep sobs shook her slender frame as she told how, taking her son, she silently slipped from the home and left the familiar neighborhood.

Traveling to another part of the country to stay with an old school friend, Lydia got a job and then rented a small place of her own. Only then did she write her father to explain why she left, and that she and her "brother" were all right.

Lydia went on to share how she came to the present school, yet wrestled with deep unrelenting guilt and shame and a fear that people would learn of her sordid past and reject both her and Joey, who was now in his early teens. She somehow couldn't shake a deep sense of uncleanness, and still struggled with feelings of hatred toward herself and her father.

Listening to her story, I was struck by the resilience of the human soul to survive such an onslaught. Again it was brought home to me the significance of the parental role in the lives of the young and innocent, who seemingly have no choice but to struggle with the bitter taste of their parents' sour grapes.

Unknown to all of us as Lydia shared, the bus her son rode to school had broken down, and Joey was lingering around back, curious about what his "sister" was learning. Amazed to see her go to the platform and begin to share, Joey had hid behind the lush foliage surrounding the pavilion and settled down to listen.

The ensuing moments became the most overwhelming of his life as he heard the full story for the first time. Listening to his "sister" share, Joey's own tears of sorrow and relief began to flow as he finally understood the mystery shrouding the early years of his life. As his mother finished, Joey could no longer control himself and ran down to the platform. Falling into the arms of his shocked mother, Joey hugged her tightly as they both wept. Quiet sobs broke the hushed silence in the pavilion as tears flowed freely down many faces watching mother and son "meet" for the first time. Finally Joey looked up at his mother, still in tears. "I always felt there was something special between you and me, and now I know why! I love you, MOM!"

THE FATHER'S BROKEN HEART

As they wept in each other's arms, it seemed God Himself hugged them in His loving paternal arms. Then one of the staff nearby felt God had a message for them. He said the Father was weeping with them in grief over how His fatherhood had been misrepresented and the agony it caused them. God wanted to tell them, the man went on, that His love was pure and undefiled and would never fail them. All of us watching felt we were on holy ground as we saw Father God reparenting mother and son, leading them to experience the truth of

His character and the beauty of His love.

At that time Lydia received a revelation of the Father which transformed her life, so much so, that she later went on to develop a powerful ministry to incest victims. She even began to share her story on TV and radio, telling how Jesus brought her to the Father and healed her through His love. Later she married a fine Christian man.

As so many of us have experienced, Lydia's picture of fatherhood had been grossly distorted by lust, also giving her a distorted view of Father God. No one has been so misrepresented, slandered, falsely accused and lied about as God the Father, a plot instigated by Satan himself. Earthly fathers have been given the role of representing Father God, yet they do everything from ignoring their children to battering them to death! It's no wonder fatherhood has come into such disrepute.

In earlier chapters we discussed the love deficit that comes into our lives as a result of a false human plumbline. By bringing us to the Father, Jesus turns this deficit into a credit, enabling us to experience the security of His love without looking for it in others. If our image of Father God remains distorted from our own negative, wounding experiences, the love deficit will only deepen in our lives.

DISTORTED IMAGES

Our need to know the true character of the Father was clearly shown to me one day when a young woman named Molly came in for counsel. Although Molly and her husband were committed Christians, they had decided to separate for a while because of conflicts in their marriage. Molly said when she was eight years old, her parents separated and she went to live with her father. One day she told her father she wanted to stay with her mother for a while, but being in poor health, he told her not to go or he would die. Torn with a desire to go and yet fearing for her dad, Molly put off the move for a time. Finally much later she did go, but to her sorrow, her father died while she was away. Now overwhelmed with pain, guilt and anguish, Molly felt her father died because she had gone against his wishes.

TRUSTING THE FATHER

For years after, Molly's only picture of Father God was this picture of her own father. Instead of trust, she had only fear of Father God, and once she married, all the old fears and mistrust surfaced. Now, while she spoke all the right Christian words, they came from her head, not her heart. Proverbs 23:7 tells us that as we think in our hearts, so we are. God brings His plumbline alongside our hearts, not our heads, because the heart determines our lifestyles and how we live.

As Molly finished, I could see the strong areas of mistrust had deeply affected her relationship with her husband. When we waited upon the Lord together, He took us back to how her father had manipulated her love with those words, and very gently, the Father ministered to her. He showed her how she had developed a lifestyle of mistrust and needed to take responsibility for her own responses by forgiving both her father and herself. Molly did so, repenting with tears, and God reached right into her being to heal the deep wound in her spirit.

What really happened in this young woman? She knew Jesus and the Holy Spirit, but she only viewed the Father with the distorted spectacles of her earthly father. That day we prayed, God released Molly from her fears and mistrust and she began the exciting discovery of Father God. Now even her marriage has been restored.

Just like Lydia and Molly, we have different pictures of Father as we come into the Christian walk. Perhaps our mother died of cancer when we were a child, or our parents divorced and sent us to a foster home. Perhaps we grew up with the devastation of an alcoholic mother, or we had a workaholic father who set a standard, yet never took time to develop that important relationship we desperately needed.

In all of these situations and more, what kind of picture would we have of Father God? What kind of plumbline would there be in our hearts? As I counsel people, I find that the plumblines they have followed are nearly always very different from God's plumbline in regards to His own character and nature.

OUR DEEPEST NEED

My own picture of Father God was that He could never really affirm or accept me, a picture greatly out of line with His plumbline. Because of my own experiences, I believed the lies of the false prophets until God ministered deeply into my life and allowed me to go on to know the Father. Only then did I begin to know true security and release.

We each need a revelation of the character and

sounds good to me 3-13-01

the nature of Father God. We know so much in our heads, and so much has been written about God - but do we know Him in our hearts? How real is He? Do we really have a deep, loving relationship with Him that's more important to us than anything else in the world?

Jesus would have us know the Father, and as we allow Him to lead us, so Father becomes a reality in our hearts and lives. Once Nehemiah allowed God, by His Spirit, to give him a revelation of his own heart, he then had a revelation of the Father's heart. Just as Nehemiah needed that revelation to accomplish the assignment God gave him, so we each need a revelation to fulfill God's purposes for us. To see the wall of salvation built up in our own lives, we must go on to know the Father. *Rog + I really need this bad.*

Our Father God is deeply grieved by the events that distort His heavenly image. He planned for His image to be reflected perfectly down through generations of families and nations, but through subtle, seductive ways, Satan, the father of lies, has turned the hearts of God's own children against Him. Many openly proclaim their mistrust, disbelief, resentment and hatred to God, even denying His very existence.

Jesus, however, steadfastly continues to be the Way to the truth and life of God our father. Only as we place our hands in His, allowing Him to lead us back into fellowship with God's loving fatherhood, can our fears and insecurities begin to melt away.

In Psalm 139, the true nature of our Father God is reflected. Outlined here, are some beautiful facets of the nature of our Father God, who is ever just in all His ways, and kind in all His deeds.

Scripture reveals Him in this Psalm as:

OMNIPOTENT	*All-powerful*	*139:1-4*
OMNIPRESENT	*All-over*	*139:5*
OMNISCIENT	*All-knowing*	*139:13-14*
OMNIPERSONAL	*All-loving*	*139:15-18*

Considering the nature of God, we can't help but be amazed at all He encompasses. If we were able to look over His shoulder and peek at His schedule for the next 24 hours, we would be awestruck at the sight of it! If we could scrutinize that schedule closely, we would find He knows the number of hairs on our head. (He must be keeping count!) But, you may ask, why would someone with such an impossible schedule involve Himself in every intricate detail of my life? I can personally only think of one reason - His love is so strong and deep toward us, no detail goes without notice.

God desires us to see Him and know Him as He really is, and He wants to give us that true revelation even more than we are ready to receive it. His heart is broken by the cruelties of parental sin, and His greatest longing is to receive His children and reveal His true character to them.

Revelation must be followed by another step. Without the next facet in our wall of salvation, such revelation can become the source of stumbling and pride. In the next chapter we will look at the greatest key to changing the lifestyle of an individual as we continue our studies in the rebuilding of the walls of salvation.

COME ASIDE

Describe the picture of Father God you formed as a child.

Describe the picture of Father God you have now.

Review the highlight times of revelation concerning His Fatherhood in your life.

God was there but distant - not personal.
Retreat situations usually brought
revelation, healing & growth.

CHAPTER 11

GOD'S STANDARD

D.L. Moody once said that the best way to prove a stick is crooked is not to denounce it or argue about it, but to lay a straight stick alongside it. In this chapter we will look at another facet of God's standard - His straight stick, representing the indestructible love of Christ and all that love embraces.

"Repent for the Kingdom of heaven is at hand."[1] These words resounded with clarity and power, electrifying crowds gathered from far and near in the wilderness. The austere figure clad in woven sackcloth of camel hair didn't mince words as he challenged everyone in the crowd to embrace God's standard. Likewise, Nehemiah had also embraced God's standard hundreds of years before

---

1. Matthew 3:2, Revised Standard Version

this event, in response to the disturbing news of his nation's devastation. After fasting and praying, Nehemiah had a revelation and repented, saying, "I confess that we, the people of Israel, have sinned. My ancestors and I have sinned."[2]

To build up the wall of salvation referred to in Isaiah 60:18, we have seen reinforcing iron rods must first be laid into the cornerstone to give a strong, stable and permanent wall. In the last chapter we saw the first rod was revelation. We will now look at the second rod of REPENTANCE.

In the process of repentance, Nehemiah considered the sins of his ancestors who went into exile because of sin. Likewise, we also need to ask who our ancestors may be, which I believe refer not only to literal ones but also to authority figures who have influenced us in significant ways. You may ask if it made a difference when Nehemiah repented for his forefathers' sins as well as his own, since most of them were dead by that time. But while waiting before the Lord, Nehemiah received not only a revelation of God the Father, but of his sins and the sins of his forefathers.

Nehemiah didn't sit in judgment, or play the "blame game," but he recognized that the sins of the fathers are visited upon the children and the children's children.[3] He saw that His ancestors or parents had eaten sour grapes, and now the bitter taste was in the children's mouths. What could he do? He took the responsibility not only for his own sins, but for all of his people and interceded before God. By doing so, Nehemiah was actually symbolizing what Jesus would later do on the cross, bearing our sin that we might be set free. If we

---

2. Nehemiah 1:6, Good News Bible
3. Numbers 14:18

also follow this biblical principle, we can change not only our own lives, but the lives of generations to come.

If Nehemiah's ancestors had responded in repentance, they and the generations to come wouldn't have been exiled to Babylon, where they remained imprisoned for years. Only by repentance, meaning a total turn around in lifestyle, can real change be brought about in our lives.

True repentance can be defined as a firm inward decision, or a change of mind. In the New Testament the English verb "to repent" is normally the translation of the Greek verb "metanoein," meaning "to change one's mind."[4] It is a decision - not an emotion.

In the Old Testament, the Hebrew word most commonly translated "to repent" literally means "to turn, to return," or "to turn back." While the New Testament emphasizes the inward nature of true repentance, the Old Testament word emphasizes the outward expression of action reflecting the inner change. Repentance, therefore, is an inner change of mind resulting in an outward turning back or around - moving in a completely new direction.

The illustration in Figure 26 shows how repentance relates to the walls of rejection and rebellion. As we have seen, we build these walls in an attempt to defend ourselves from various assailants in our lives. When we repent of sin, the walls come down, and we are able to build the wall of salvation according to God's Divine Plumbline.

---

4. W.E. Vine, The Expanded Vine's Expository Dictionary of New Testament Words, (Minneapolis:Bethany House Publishers, 1984), pp. 251-252.

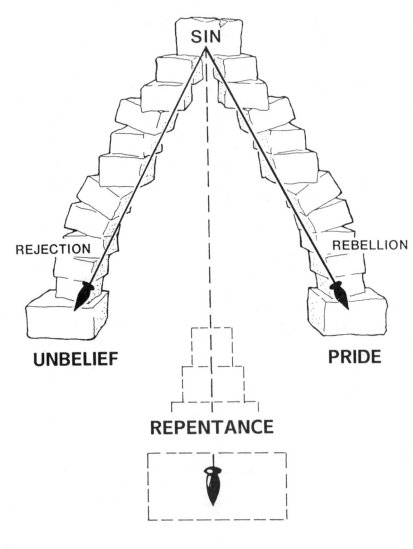

FIGURE 26

How does rejection relate to sin in our heritage? We are not accountable for the rejection imposed on us during our childhood, but if we receive negative input that devalues us and then continue in that frame of reference, that is when our accountability begins. The ensuing battle from unbelief toward faith then becomes one between the truth of the Lord and the programming we received in our upbringing.

DETERMINING VALUE

To illustrate this dynamic, let us consider the value of a Casio wristwatch. We speak of its value in terms of the price paid, as we generally do for all items. But what about the value of life? More specifically, what is the value of *your* life?

When I once asked this question at a medical seminar in Switzerland, one doctor said, "I'm worth 20 Swiss francs plus gold fillings." According to research, he explained, that's all our bodies are worth! We all laughed, until another doctor spoke up. "No, no, we're worth two million Swiss Franks because we Swiss work so hard!"

Dr. Harold J. Morowitz, a professor of molecular biophysics, calculated the average value of a gram of human being and concluded he was worth $6,000,015.44. So he himself was the Six Million Dollar Man! Even after his "average man" research, Dr. Morowitz concluded, "How would we assemble the cells into tissues, tissues into organs and organs into persons?"

The very task staggers the imagination. Now our ability to ask the question in dollars and cents has immediately disappeared! We sharply face the realization that each human being is priceless. We are led from a lowly pile of common materials to this grand philosophical conclusion - every person is infinitely precious. The psalmist arrived at the same conclusion as he pondered how he was "woven together" in his mother's womb: "I am fearfully and wonderfully made."[5]

As we honestly ponder the value of our lives, we need to look at our price, and who is the buyer. The Bible tells us we are not our own for we were bought with a price![6] Our calenders still confirm that Christ died almost 2000 years ago, laying down His life on a cruel cross to purchase us with His own life's blood, saving us from sin and death. No human currency can measure the price that He paid. The Bible says: "Greater love has no one than this, that one lay down his life for his friends."[7] Viewing this fact, we each as individuals must grasp this truth: **we are priceless in value.**

SEEING OUR WORTH

"None of them can by any means redeem [either himself or] his brother, nor give to God a ransom for him - For the ransom of a life is too costly, and [the price one can pay] can never suffice."[8] God is clearly telling us that all the wealth in the world could never buy a single one of us. Only the blood of Jesus can. Our value in the sight of God is more than all the wealth of this world. For us to say we are unworthy, inferior, or without value, is not to speak from God's point of view.

---

5. Psalm 139:14, New International Version
6. 1 Corinthians 6:19-20
7. John 15:13, New International Version
8. Psalm 49:7-8, Amplified Bible

When I've asked students if they feel priceless, very few respond affirmatively. When asked if they have ever told themselves they are priceless, fewer still answered positively. What does this show us? Unbelief residing in the heart negates God's perspective on our true value and worth. Misbelief, or unbelief, is the most significant sin in rejection.

Many of us find it easier to agree with our parental and societal programming and the deeply entrenched emotions that reinforce it, than to agree with God's love for us. By believing such lies, we actually have indulged in the sin of unbelief. Even hidden unbelief residing in our hearts negates God's true perspective on our priceless value, making His love seem only a distant theory to our hearts. By wallowing in unbelief, we have actually concurred with our old, human plumbline of rejection and failed to embrace the Divine Plumbline.

Success or accomplishments don't determine the worth of a person, and neither do performance, achievement or even the number of people who love and respect us. Our worth is based totally, and solely, on the declaration of God: "For God so loved the world ..."[9] Nothing can change this fact.

THE SIN OF UNBELIEF

Unbelief first began in the garden of Eden when Satan found a way to deceive Eve into questioning God. Still as deceptive today, unbelief remains the cardinal sin or foundation stone upon which each block in the wall of rejection is laid. Both the "Compliant" and "Can't Do It" personalities we discussed in chapter seven have their base in

---

9. John 3:16

unbelief.

The sin of unbelief was so serious in God's eyes, a generation of Israelites was disqualified from entering the land promised to them as their inheritance.[10] Only Joshua and Caleb dared to believe, while the others, doubting God's provision, perished in the wilderness.

Today, many fail to receive their inheritance for the same reason - unbelief. Life for them is wandering in the wilderness, plagued by doubts, misgivings, discouragement, self-rejection and even self-hatred. Unable to attain their goals, dreams and desires, they are lost in the wilderness of disillusionment and doubt.

THE SIN OF REBELLION

When the plumbline of rebellion is the reference point for a person's life, he builds his wall of rebellion with the cardinal sin of pride as the cornerstone. The "Competitive" and "Critical" personalities are based in the pride of life, defined as an unwillingness to be known for who we really are, or projecting ourselves to be someone we are not. God resists pride,[11] and eventually He will bring it to an end.[12] Sometimes people feel God is not only against them but is also resisting them, when in actuality God is resisting the pride they refuse to let go.

Take Jack, for example. After becoming a Christian and handing his business over to God, Jack experienced crisis after crisis. His family relationships deteriorated as rifts developed between

---

10. Hebrews 3:16-19
11. 1 Peter 5:5
12. Isaiah 2:12, New International version

he and his wife. Finally Jack's life went from bad to worse when a major setback affected both his business and his family. Jack began to see that God was dealing with the pride in his life at many different levels. As he began to co-operate with God and deal with pride, Jack's circumstances changed. Soon he found a new perspective on life. What Jack discovered was central to our walk with God. He turned the key that would free him from false human plumblines by beginning to humble himself.

To discern if pride is also in your life, ask yourself the following questions:

When someone is chosen in the position you wanted, or if someone's gifts and accomplishments outshine yours - how do you react? Are you jealous? Angry?

In our moments of honest self-criticism, we say many things about ourselves. How do you react when someone else says the same things about you?

When you are criticized, does it arouse hostility and resentment? Do you justify yourself and criticize the critic?

If you see areas in your own life which you've built on the cornerstone of pride, you, like Jack, need to turn the key of humility. Defined as the willingness to be known for who we are in spite of the consequences, humility is the key that opens the door for God's grace to freely work in our lives.[13] As we walk transparently into the truth and light,

---

13. 1 Peter 5:5-6

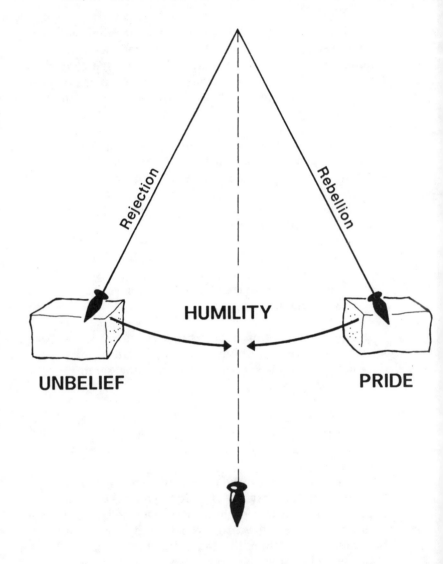

FIGURE 27

both of which are liberating, we discover humility in our lives.

UNDERSTANDING HUMILITY

Humility is also a quality of love. If we say we love God but don't love our brother or sister, then, as the scripture says, "How can the love of God be in him?"[14] Just as my love for God is evidenced by my love for my brother and sister, so my humility toward God is evidenced through my relationship with others. Instead of cringing and drawing back from humility, we need to be willing to be known for who we really are.

One day in prayer I asked the Lord, "Why is it so difficult for me to let people know who I am, yet it's so easy to let You know who I am?" These words softly formed in my mind: "It's because you fear man more than you fear Me." Surprised, I knew it was true. Afraid of rejection and being wounded, I often struggled to reveal who I really was for fear of what others would say and think. For the first time I saw true repentance involves true humility, that willingness to be known for who I really am.

The Greek word for humility is "tapeinos", meaning "low-lying in spirit, of low degree in spirit, abased."[15] None of us enjoys being abased, but if we walk in humility, we need to embrace abasing. Who lives in the presence of God? Psalm 51:17 says it's he who has a "broken and a contrite heart." That person is the one who dwells there with God in a high and holy place, because our

---

14. 1 John 3:17, New International version
15. Vine's Expository Dictionary, op. cit., pp. 568-569

abasing, or being cast low, is God's key to our being exalted. Repentance is a process that should never stop. We must continually experience brokenness before God over the sinfulness of our hearts. How can we walk daily in this experience? James 5:16-17 in the Amplified Bible says:

"Confess to one another therefore your faults (your slips, your false steps, your offenses, your sins) and pray [also] for one another, that you may be healed and restored [to a spiritual tone of mind and heart]. The earnest (heartfelt, continued) prayer of a righteous man makes tremendous power available [dynamic in its working].

We need to come to the Lord repenting of our unbelief and pride, as well as all their fruits, while we exercise our hearts in humility before Him. Then, as we begin to open our hearts and lives to share with another individual, so God will begin an unprecedented healing process in our lives. But the first step is a willingness to be vulnerable and to confess our faults, failings and sins to someone with whom we have established some degree of trust and relationship. Of course, with deep, difficult issues, it is advisable to share with someone who has had training in Christian counseling, and believes in the power of prayer to heal and restore.

So, as we've seen, the challenge Nehemiah gives us is to sink that reinforcing rod of repentance deeply into the foundation stone of redemption. To facilitate the ongoing process of healing and restoration, it is essential to continually walk in the light with one another.

As we build the wall of salvation, there are

still some significant reinforcing rods that are essential to building a structure strong enough to withstand the storms of our times. In the next chapter we will look at how repentance, as a process, can transform our lifestyle, and, through faith, release all the resources of the Godhead.

COME ASIDE

Review any areas of unbelief and pride in your life.

Evaluate the effectiveness of your repentance in these or other areas.

CHAPTER 12

TORMENTED HEART

Now that we have examined the inception of repentance, we will continue to examine it as a process changing our lifestyle. We will see how biblical repentance exceeds all other approaches to change, and how when we use faith as the activating key it opens the door to all the resources of the Godhead.

The first significant component of repentance is found in relation to the cross. Jesus said: "If anyone would come after me, he must deny himself and take up his cross daily and follow me."[1] All too many of us fail to embrace God's challenge to apply this truth. What did Jesus mean by this statement? Figure 28 depicts how we can flow from the old man to the new, with Adam representing the epitomy of the unbelief and pride

---

1. Luke 9:23, New International Version

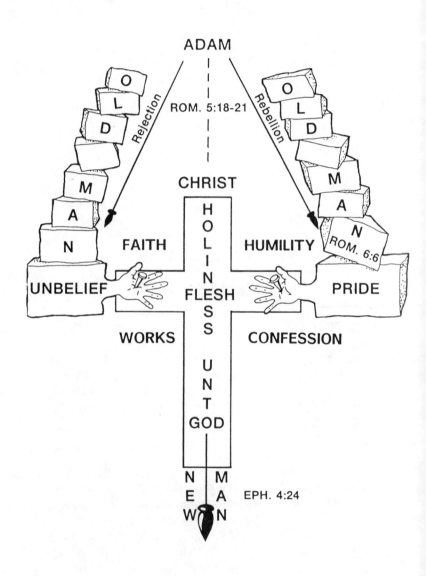

FIGURE 28

we inherit and acquire in life. The only way to effectively forsake unbelief and pride is by nailing them to the cross, along with all the sins Christ bore there. To do this, we must first reckon ourselves to be dead indeed to these areas in our lives. Secondly, we must replace unbelief by receiving God's declaration of our true value and grasping by faith the truth about ourselves. Finally, we must proceed to live it out.

James says, "Faith without works is dead."[2] A mere intellectual assent of truth is of little value without daily application. Faith's outworking is very important. It moves us from the plumbline of rejection to one of self-acceptance and worth, which is in line with God's plumbline. If we need to move from the platform of pride, the keys to change are humility and confession. Confessing our sins unlocks the deep issues of the heart, and humility holds the door open for heart change to occur. Through transparency, we deal a death blow to the root of pride. When we apply the humility of confession, pride is stripped of its power, no longer able to control our lives. The challenge we are given is to put off the old, unwanted elements of pride and unbelief and to put on new, desired ones.[3] We are not talking about mental acrobatics, but a release of power, bringing change through the victory won on the cross. Faith in Christ's finished work releases victory to the individual who truly exercises that faith.

As we make these changes, we will meet some inner resistance, as illustrated in Figure 29. In this illustration, we see the engine represents the SPIRIT, the coal car represents the MIND, and the

---

2. James 2:20
3. Colossians 3:8-10

FIGURE 29

caboose represents the EMOTIONS. Satan engineers his ride from the EMOTIONS caboose, making the most of how we live in our existential, contemporary western world. Instead of allowing us to be guided by principle and truth, Satan masterfully manipulates us into allowing feelings to direct and even control us. Emotions are important and helpful communicators, but they are extremely dangerous dictators. They were given to be under our control, not to become our task masters!

EMOTIONS OUT OF CONTROL

Perhaps we've seen someone like the young man who stormed out in a fit of rage, climbed onto his motorcycle and roared off at high speed. Newspapers the next morning published the rest of the story beneath the headline: "Four Killed In Head-on Collision At High Speed." Likewise, when we allow our emotions to control us, we are heading for disaster. All over the western world, we see the tragic effects of emotions out of control. Many nations report suicide as the number one killer of their youth. Depression has reached epidemic proportions, demonstrating the effects of its control on a society that gives it that liberty!

The next illustration in Figure 30 will help us understand the powerful opposition we face as we attempt to repent, or turn around.

The train at the top of the illustration, which could be called the "humanistic train," indicates our state as we follow the leadership of our emotions. The train below represents the position of balance we desire, when our human spirit is led by God's Holy Spirit and the emotions follow behind. But what happens as the changeover occurs?

TRAINS OF LIFE

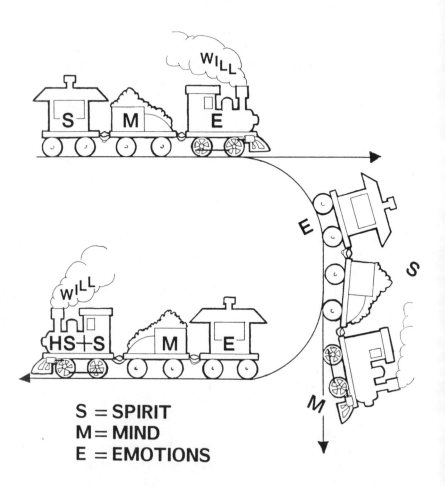

S = SPIRIT
M = MIND
E = EMOTIONS

FIGURE 30

As depicted in the train straining to round the bend, our emotions will claw like a cornered cat, spitting, snarling and growling in menacing defense. If the process is not stopped, they may even threaten to give us an emotional breakdown, since they are so insecure and angry about losing their control over us.

When we look at the Hebrew word translated as repentance, we gain understanding of why this happens. This word "nawkham" literally means "sighing, groaning, gasping and shaking," all these reflecting deep, passionate upheaval. In essence, that's what happens to our emotions when we are in repentance. When we finally round the bend, (if we make it,) our emotions will eventually experience joy, directed by the Holy Spirit.

In the same way, a "rationalistic train" powered by the mind presents a similar situation. Then as we try to repent, the great battle we wage is with "reasoned" resistance to repentance. The fear of appearing foolish, childish or irrational, could be a forceful opponent to our changing.

RATIONALISTIC TRAIN

A third unbalanced option we could face is to have our human spirit guiding out in front, but still under the influence of something other than the Holy Spirit. This can be called a "spiritualistic" or "occult train." During repentance, prayer for deliverance from evil spirits could be necessary for such an individual, and the opposition from the enemy can sometimes be volatile or dramatic.

SPIRITUALISTIC TRAIN

Although we have separated these different facets represented by the trains of the emotions, mind, or spirit, all three may be present in varying combinations. As John the Baptist warned us to repent for the kingdom of heaven is at hand,[4] so we must repent to experience true change of heart and life. The more we build our lives in line with the Divine Plumbline, the more of life we truly will be able to live.

---

4. Matthew 3:2

BEING RELEASED

To experience change, we will now look at another aspect of repentance which is so important, that without it, repentance would be null and void. In chapter one of Nehemiah, we find an account of a remarkable relationship between slave and king, between Jew and Gentile master, and between the oppressed and his oppressor.

When Nehemiah heard the news of Jerusalem, his sadness was reflected in his countenance when he appeared before the king. Nehemiah's role as the king's cupbearer was to bring the king both cheer and good wine. For Nehemiah to allow his grief to show in the king's presence meant he placed himself in danger of death. But Nehemiah's concern for his people outweighed his self interest, and when King Artaxerxes observed his sorrowful countenance, he asked him to explain.

What follows reflects a deep love on the part of the King for his cupbearer Nehemiah. When the King heard about the state of Jerusalem, he not only released Nehemiah from his palace duties, but gave him permission and provision to restore the Holy City! This not only shows God's hand in supporting Nehemiah, but also reveals the depths of Nehemiah's heart. Obviously he had come to the place where he'd freely forgiven his enemies, and was even able to faithfully and loyally serve their king. He had RELEASED his oppressors from their sins against his people, and no residual resentment or bitterness remained in his heart. This, then, is the next reinforcing rod to be sunk into the foundation stone of redemption: RELEASE.

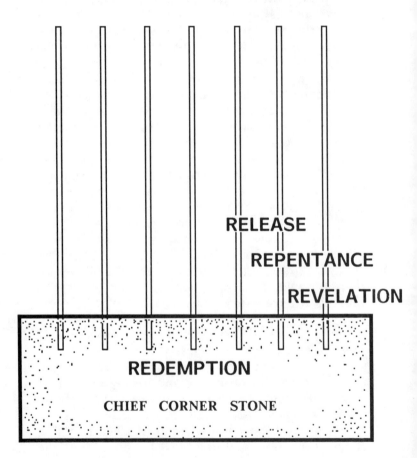

FIGURE 31

Forgiving someone who has offended us RELEASES him from needing to repay us, give compensation, or even say he is sorry. When we do come to the place of forgiving from the heart, another kind of release happens simultaneously within us. Let me illustrate this by the following story.

During our YWAM counseling schools, time is given for students to share from their own lives. Kay, a woman in her late forties, began to tell us about who she was, but after only a few minutes fell silent. When two of us went over and quietly prayed for her, suddenly Kay began to shake, railing at us with verbal and even physical abuse. We immediately recognized that we were not dealing with an ordinary release of emotion, but were encountering demonic influences. As we intensified our prayers, her reactions increased. After some time with no change, we decided to meet with Kay again after class.

Later, while waiting in prayer, one of us received a word of knowledge from the Lord that Kay was not willing to forgive her mother. When we challenged her about it, she acknowledged a deep root of bitterness in her heart, and began shouting, "I hate you! I hate you! I hate you!" as if her mother was in the room.

RELEASING FORGIVENESS

As we talked together, at last Kay came to the place where she was willing to release forgiveness to her mother. When we prayed for her again, Kay was immediately set free from the tormenters that had hid behind her unforgiveness.

In the Gospel of Matthew,[5] the story is told of

---

5. Matthew 18:21-35

RELEASE THROUGH
FORGIVENESS

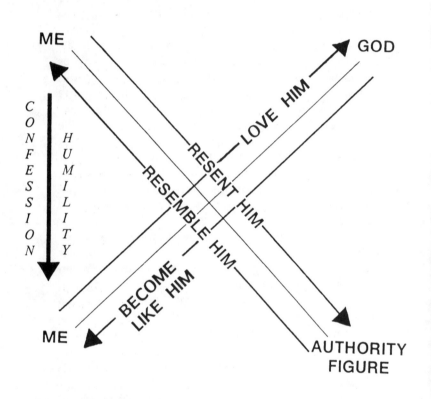

FIGURE 32

a man who was forgiven a debt of "$10 million" but neglected to forgive as he was forgiven. While traveling home he met a fellow servant owing him a paltry "$20." Instead of showing mercy as he had received mercy, he had the man cast into jail. When the first man's creditor heard of it, he was furious, and retracted his original kindness by handing him over to the tormentors until he paid the full "$10 million." Now the man was in jail not for his original debt, but for his brutality and unforgiving spirit. Jesus concluded the parable saying that God will do the same to each of us if we fail to forgive our brother from the heart.

We draw from this story, then, that unforgiveness provides a platform for inner torment. We are not designed to live with resentment, bitterness or hatred. To continue in them invites spiritual as well as physical ailments to develop within. To further elaborate, let's look at Figure 32.

BECOMING A REPLICA

We see in this illustration that an unforgiving attitude often results from some injustice, either real or imagined, in childhood. As we grow up, we may have a negative focus on that authority figure, which is then reflected in our adolescence.

The transition from a focus on an earthly authority figure to God is only facilitated through humility and confession. Resentment needs to be confessed and the offender unconditionally forgiven. This is the beginning of release and a new focus.

One morning while working in our counseling clinic in Hawaii, a young man named Neville visited me. Recently married, Neville shared he

SEEING GOD CLEARLY

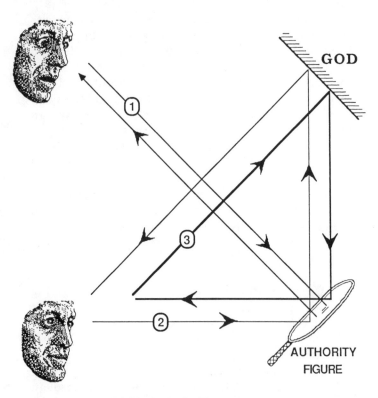

1. Seeing Authority Figure
2. Seeing God though Authority Figure
3. Seeing God

FIGURE 33

was already experiencing marital problems. As he wept, he confessed that he despised and resented his father for destroying his family through alcoholism. But now, to Neville's dismay and horror, he found himself in the same battle with the bottle his father had faced.

When we condemn another, passing judgment in our hearts, a dangerous dynamic occurs, and we find ourselves in the same sin that we judged. Take for example Jane, who, as a victim of incest, judged in her heart that all men were alike as far as sex was concerned. To them, she felt, women were to be used and if necessary abused, simply to satisfy their own desires. This dynamic began when, after making a judgment, Jane became like those she hated by using and abusing men through prostitution. Her judging and resentment had become like a boomerang, coming back at her because she was convinced all men were alike, tarred with the same brush. The only love she really knew was lust.

THE ONLY ANSWER

As we've discussed, the only way out of such a destructive spiral is walking through *humility* and *confession*. First we must be open and honest about our resentments, then extend forgiveness without qualifications. Speaking out that forgiveness, often a difficult step, can become the start of forgiveness from the heart.

Often our biggest task is to forgive ourselves. But through such forgiveness, the woundings of the heart are healed as bitter tears are wept. Scars can't be completely removed, and tear stains on the delicate fabric of our emotions are, more often than not, permanent. But those who are too stubborn to forgive, unknowingly choose torment.

Even after taking the step of forgiveness, we may struggle to be free from projecting our fears and mistrust onto God as pictured in Figure 33. Often we still have a strong tendency to see God through the distorted picture of our earthly authority figures (path #2). Instead of looking through this "authority figure" mirror for understanding and wisdom, we need to look directly at God (path #3) for the reflection of our true image.

The more we see God as He really is, the more we love Him and begin to resemble Him (Figure 32). This release comes to us through forgiveness when we give it unconditionally, or, as in the words of Jesus, when we forgive up to 70 x 7 times!

As we have seen, tormentors find their chance to harass us and even destroy us if they can, all through refusing to forgive. In the next chapter we will face our tormenters as they battle against Nehemiah, whose skill and wisdom disarm them again and again.

COME ASIDE

Review the type of trains you caught in life.

Relate some of your experiences in repentance.

Describe any "torment" you have experienced through unforgiveness. What steps brought you out of it?

CHAPTER 13

ROUTING OUR ENEMY

The greatest opponent to rebuilding the walls of salvation in our lives is Lucifer himself. Some regard him as a figment of the imagination, while others see him as the lord of the world who will one day be worshipped as such. However he is viewed, Satan still remains a formidable foe with a mean track record! The Bible clearly states that Satan is alive and active in this world, with a multitude of followers locked in his grasp, who, as the end of this age draws near, will give him increasing allegiance and authority. It is also during this time that the love of many Christians will grow cold.[1]

Nehemiah also faced the wiles of the enemy as he obeyed the call of God to rebuild Jerusalem's walls. Looking at his struggles, we will recognize some of Satan's strategies to deter and defeat the

---

1. Matthew 24:11-13

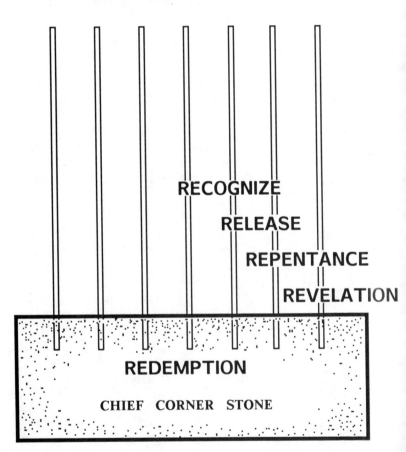

FIGURE 34

God-given plans of Nehemiah. We will see that the next reinforcing rod to be sunk into the chief cornerstone is RECOGNIZE. In dealing with Satan, before anything else, we must learn how to recognize his strategies so we can destroy his operations.

ANGER AND FEAR

In Nehemiah 4:1-7, we read that Satan's major agents were Sanballat, Geshem and Tobiah, who responded in anger when they heard of Nehemiah's plans to restore Jerusalem's walls. Meeting him as he traveled to the city, they assailed him with threats and accusations. While many of Nehemiah's predecessors and descendants gave in to fear and intimidation, Nehemiah refused to be deterred.

"Fear of man will prove to be a snare, but whoever trusts in the Lord is kept safe."[2] Nehemiah not only believed, but lived in the truth of this word, trusting the Lord.

Just as Nehemiah found, Satan will hurl his fury at us through loved ones, equipment failure, adverse circumstances, governments, illness, mental and physical breakdowns, and many other ways. But Joseph, Job, and especially Jesus are excellent examples of how God turns Satan's wrath to His advantage. Stephen was stoned by angry men fueled by Satan himself - but if Satan had known the power he was unleashing, he would have stopped in his tracks. Standing by was Saul, about to become Paul the apostle, and Stephen's death

2. Proverbs 29:25, New International Version

demonstrated a quality of forgiveness that shook Saul to the core.

"God did not give us a spirit of timidity - of cowardice, of fawning fear - but He has given us a spirit of power and of love and of a calm and well balanced mind."[3] Satan tries to intimidate us through fear, but to those who trust, the enemy's roar is like a toothless lion unable to devour.

MOCKING

Another strategy of the enemy is *mocking,* which also arises out of a person's suppressed hostility. Nehemiah's enemies scorned and taunted him, falsely accusing him of rebelling against King Artaxerxes,[4] who had already given his blessing on the task. Sanballat even accused Nehemiah of trying to bribe God![5] Here a subtle attack is waged on Nehemiah's own ground, similar to Satan's tactic with Jesus when he misquoted scripture to Him in the wilderness.[6] By taking truth and turning it around in this way, Satan has at times divided the church and weakened its effectiveness by severing unity - just as he subtly tried to do to Nehemiah.

While Sanballat mocked the task as hopelessly futile, Tobiah tried to undermine the group's skills and abilities. But he had forgotten that most of them had lived in captivity under forced labor for years, building bricks and walls! Truthfulness is not important to the "accuser of the brethren." His whole purpose in mocking is to bring us to a place of doubt and unbelief, aborting the purposes and plans of God for our lives.

interesting

---

3. 2 Timothy 1:7, Amplified Bible
4. Nehemiah 2:19
5. Nehemiah 4:1-3

As I travel around the world conducting many seminars and speaking in schools, I often see Satan at work - but there is one encounter I will never forget. Maida had been ensnared by lust and wounded through many intimate relationships with men in her search for love. Sadly, I have seen countless people like Maida enter the marriage bed with pounds of excess baggage. Before they can really experience deep fulfillment and intimacy, they must unload the weights from the past. The excess baggage is often carried into their new relationship with Christ, and can also seriously hinder the development of intimacy with God.

help

Maida was no exception, and we explained this to her. But as we prayed with her to be free from the encumbrances of her old lifestyle, suddenly Maida's body went into convulsions. The next thing that happened, showed us clearly that demons were battling to keep control.

The corners of her mouth curled in a mocking sneer, and a strange voice belittled our attempts to help her. The sneering, mocking laughter that escaped her lips sent shivers down our spines. By then we knew Satan's platform was deeply entrenched in Maida's life and he was not about to let her go without a struggle. Over the following weeks, with a couple of my staff, I continued to counsel and pray with Maida. Each time as the enemy mocked us, we encouraged her to take the responsibility and renounce his evil works in her life. Gradually, Maida's spiritual strength grew, until she found herself with a new authority over the powers of darkness.

_____(continued)

6. Matthew 4:3,6

CONFUSION AND DECEPTION

Other favorite approaches the father of lies uses to throw us off balance and out of action include *confusion and deception.*

In Nehemiah 4:8, Sanballat, Geshem and Tobiah plotted with neighboring allies to injure, confuse and deceive the Jewish restorers. But in spite of many attempts, Nehemiah steadfastly refused to succumb to their deceptions and remained trusting in God, completing the work on the walls. We need to recognize that Satan is the author of confusion. When clouds of confusion gather overhead, we must wait until the wind of God's Spirit blows the clouds away, allowing the sun to shine brightly and give clear direction on our path. Nehemiah tells of a prophetess named Noadiah and several others[7] who, through *false prophecy,* tried to intimidate and turn Nehemiah aside from God's call to rebuild Jerusalem's walls.

As we have discussed in previous chapters, Satan can use such *false prophets* to sway us from God's truth. Such attacks can be very devastating, especially if they come through a spouse, parent or church member. Sometimes we may feel like Job, whose wife advised him "to curse God and die" during the most vulnerable crisis of his life. [8]

We do not want to be like the young prophet in 1 Kings 13 either, who took the advice of an older prophet rather than what God had said, and fell into the jaws of a lion as a result. We need to be discerning, and watch and pray so as not to be led astray.

---

7. Nehemiah 6:14
8. Job 2:9

FALSE FRIENDS

False friendships, another snare of the enemy, can easily be made, but just as easily will betray. The priest Eliashib betrayed Nehemiah while he was gone by giving his enemy Tobiah a large chamber in the temple to use as a bedroom.[9] This story depicts a classic strategy of Satan, who in the same way uses our relationships with the world to establish a place of operation in our hearts. We cannot love both the world and God, because friendship with the world is enmity with God.[10]

As we read on in Nehemiah chapter 13, we note that Nehemiah immediately confronted Eliashib's compromise by throwing all of Tobiah's belongings out in the street. Likewise, we also must act without compromise or mercy toward the enemy, for he will certainly have no mercy on us. As a devouring adversary, Satan's assignment is to ensnare our hearts. Through false allegiances he has maligned many lives and powerful ministries.

DEMONIC INFLUENCE

The ultimate goal of Satan is to *demonize* us by seducing us into forming evil alliances with a great variety of agencies, people and desires. The word "demonize" is the more literal translation from the New Testament Greek word "daimonizomai," which means to be influenced by a demon or to act under its control.[11] To be "demonized" simply refers to

---

9. Nehemiah 13:4-9
10. 1 John 2:15-16
11. Vine's Expository Dictionary, op.cit., p.238

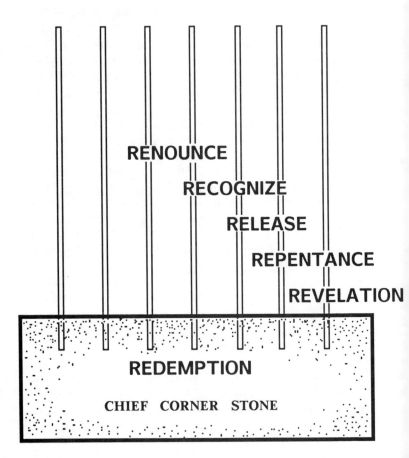

FIGURE 35

the process Satan uses to establish himself in our hearts and ultimately take over. The greater access we allow him, the more he will assume, and consequently the greater authority he will retain in our lives. When we sense Satan's influence or presence in any place of our hearts, we must immediately emulate the actions of Nehemiah and give him no ground on which to stand. Don't think of entertaining him for a minute! Guard and keep your heart with *all* diligence, because out of your heart flow the issues of your life.[12]

RENOUNCE

Now that we have looked at some wicked stratagems of the enemy to guard against, we need to ask how to deal with the enemy once we have discovered his presence? As we've discussed the first step to annulling the activity of Satan in our lives is to recognize his work. The second step to dealing with him is to renounce him and all of his activity in our lives. This, then, is the reinforcing rod to be sunk next into the foundation stone - RENOUNCE.

NEHEMIAH WAITED ON GOD

From the time he first heard about the state of Jerusalem, we find Nehemiah seeking the Lord with fasting and prayer. Later, when he heard his enemies were plotting against him, Nehemiah went straight to prayer and set a watch.[13] When Shemaiah was hired to trick Nehemiah into hiding

12. Proverbs 4:23
13. Nehemiah 1:4; 4:9

in the temple just to get him out of the way, Nehemiah saw through the plot and placed his enemies in the hands of the Lord.

At what stage during a crisis do we seek the Lord, if at all? Like Nehemiah, we need to seek Him *immediately* and draw from the greatest resource available for any situation. The enemy may easily outwit us at times, but he is no match for our God!

NEHEMIAH WALKED ON, FEARING THE LORD

Nehemiah's enemies tried to intimidate and frighten him from continuing to build the walls of Jerusalem.[14] But Nehemiah didn't fear for his own life, having entrusted that to God. Instead his greatest fear was not pleasing the Lord. Nehemiah stood in awe of God, acknowledging what God commanded him to do, rather than fearing men. "Fear of man will prove to be a snare, but whoever trusts in the Lord is kept safe."[15] If we fear anything more than we fear the awesome, Almighty God, we will fall into the snare of the fear of man. If we value man's opinions, assessments, advice, or ideas of ourselves or situations, more than we value those of God, we are already trapped in the fear of man. God is the only remedy for fear. "The fear of the Lord [the acknowledgement of who He is, and the hatred of evil] is the beginning of wisdom."[16] According to scripture, Nehemiah repeatedly showed himself to be a man of wisdom.

Do we succumb to the fear of man and so fall

---

14. Nehemiah 6:8-14
15. Proverbs 29:25, New International Version
16. Proverbs 1:7, Amplified Bible

into its snare? When we are overcome by fear, we are believing that whoever, or whatever, we fear is stronger and greater than God. No one is greater or mightier than Him.

NEHEMIAH KEPT WORKING ON

In Nehemiah 4:1,7 we read how upset Sanballat and Tobiah became when someone held the welfare of the Jews in mind. But even in the face of such opposition, Nehemiah continued to survey the rubble that once represented the proud, sturdy walls of Jerusalem. He refused to be distracted from the work God called him to do. Even the mockery of his noisy enemies could not deter him, and, having committed his situation to the Lord, he continued to build and encourage his co-workers to do likewise.

The threat of war did not stop the work from continuing either.[17] Working together to finish the walls, half the men held on to their spears in case fighting broke out, and the rest labored on. Just as they were, we too need to be ready to fight as we work, because we have an enemy who will stop at nothing to prevent God from building His church. But even the forces of hell will eventually succumb to the might and power of the Living God. We need to imitate Nehemiah, who, in the face of the most adverse circumstances and unappreciative advisors, kept working on toward the goal. Let us be "steadfast, unmovable, always abounding in the work of the Lord ..."[18]

---

17. Nehemiah 4:21
18. 1 Corinthians 15:58, King James Version

NEHEMIAH WATCHED FOR THE ENEMY

"But we prayed to our God and posted a guard day night to meet this threat. ... Neither I nor my brothers, nor my men, nor the guards with me took off our clothes; each had his weapon, even when he went for water."[19]

Nehemiah not only waited on God, but guarded against any deterrents to keep them from doing the will of God. The enemy may come clothed as an angel of light or as a stalking lion, but his intentions are always to stop the work of God in us and through us. Through unawareness, many have fallen before his cunning tactics, but if we emulate Nehemiah, we will watch and pray that we enter not into temptation.

NEHEMIAH WITHDREW

Nehemiah was challenged by a Horonite, an Ammonite and an Arabian.[20] They ridiculed and despised the Jews, accusing them of rebelling against the king in order to frighten them from completing the work.

How did Nehemiah respond? He withdrew, refusing to deal with his accusers by saying they had no right or portion in the city, and must disassociate themselves from the entire enterprise.

Later, Tobiah's presence in the temple stirred Nehemiah into action.[21] Once again he separated himself from his enemies by purging the temple of Tobiah's possessions, and kept himself from the in-

---

19. Nehemiah 4:9; 4:23, New International Version
20. Nehemiah 2:19
21. Nehemiah 13:7-9

fluence of evil men.

There is a time to confront, as well as withdraw and separate ourselves from the influence of evil over our lives. Peer group pressure overpowers many Christians who linger too long under its influence. Even King Saul knelt before the pressure of his peers and as a result lost his leadership over Israel.[22] Other kings and judges also failed to leave their allegiances with the enemy, and as a result failed to fulfill their calling. There is a time to embrace and a time to refrain from embracing.[23] The challenge we continually face is to discern the right response for our immediate circumstance.

NEHEMIAH WARRED ON

The Jew's enemies threatened to come and kill them as they worked on the wall. As we already discussed, their threats didn't deter Nehemiah but instead prepared him for battle. Half the men and some of the families were to stand guard fully armed, while the others worked on, armed with swords.

Not only do we see here Nehemiah's determination to work on, but his recognition of the need to *war on*. Nehemiah knew something we all must come to grips with - the fact that we are at war. We all have an enemy waiting to overcome us, who will only make peace on his terms. The only way to win is to become first-class soldiers equipped by Christ, not entangled with the affairs of this life, but committed to watching, battling and building under His leadership.[24]

---

22. 1 Samuel 14:13-15
23. Ecclesiastes 3:5
24. 1 Timothy 2:3-4

Because our warfare is fought not so much in the physical realm but in the unseen spiritual world, our weapons must be fitted for this kind of battle. Paul says these weapons are not carnal, but mighty to pull down the enemy's strongholds.[25] Let's look at some of these weapons and how to wield them.

THE NAME OF JESUS

When we use the name of Jesus, we align ourselves with His forces, fighting for truth, justice and righteousness. There is power in His name above all the power of the enemy.[26]

THE BLOOD OF JESUS

In Revelation 12:11 we read "they overcame by the blood of the lamb," speaking of the great victory Jesus won on the cross over sin, death and the devil. When Jesus shed his life's blood, He did so in our place, providing a way for us to be saved out of the devil's domination. His blood was shed on our behalf and before it the enemy fled.

THE WORD OF OUR TESTIMONY

The other weapon for victory mentioned in Revelation 12:11 is the "word of our testimony." While fasting in the wilderness for forty days, Jesus demonstrated this power of the Word as He battled the devil's temptations.[27] Expertly wielding the

---

25. 2 Corinthians 10:3-5
26. Luke 10:19; Philippians 2:9-10; Ephesians 1:21
27. Matthew 4:1-11

Word like a sword, Jesus set the enemy to flight instead of yielding to his temptations. God's Word is truth. As we believe His Word and confess it before our enemy, that truth will make us free.[28]

THE ARMOR OF GOD

Ephesians chapter 6 tells us to put on the whole armor of God so we can stand in the day of battle against powers of darkness. Each piece of armor is important:

> *The helmet of salvation;*
> *The breastplate of righteousness;*
> *The belt of truth;*
> *The shoes of the gospel;*
> *The shield of faith; and*
> *The sword of the Spirit.*

If we put on this armor daily, and learn to employ it, we will be able to drive the enemy back, again and again.

A few years ago, several of us were praying with an elderly man who had suicidal tendencies. A simple prayer time suddenly exploded into a hair-raising event with the enemy exposing himself as the vicious taskmaster he is. The elderly man jumped up with a roar, uttering deep guttural growls as his face contorted with anger. Grabbing a chair and holding it over his head, he slowly started moving toward us in the electrified room. One of our group stood frozen with fear, but others of us seized our weapons of spiritual warfare. Calling on the name of Jesus and proclaiming the

---

28. John 8:32

power of His blood, we watched as the man suddenly stopped a few feet from us, held by unseen hands. Then the chair crashed to the floor, and with a scream the man slumped onto the carpet, sobbing like a child.

As we knelt beside him he confessed the adultery in his life, repenting before the Lord. Then we agreed in prayer with him as he renounced the works of the enemy in his life, at last winning the release he so desired. We later found the man's insomnia, depression and suicidal thoughts were short-lived as he continued in the victory, standing against the dominion of the evil one in his life.

The devil is indeed a formidable foe, as we have seen in his attack against Nehemiah. In the next chapter, we will consider another approach of the enemy altogether. Injustice, real or imagined, is difficult to deal with, especially when it enters our lives from people we trusted. Satan knows how to use this sword, and has cut down many with its blade. We will go on to see how we can not only avoid these thrusts of the enemy, but actually disarm him of this weapon.

COME ASIDE

Review some of the major satanic attacks you have had in your life.

Illustrate from your own life how you have used some of Nehemiah's strategies to defeat Satan.

CHAPTER 14

A FRESH START

Injustice upon injustice, thrust upon the Israelites from within their ranks and without, gave them much hurt and wounding as they eked out a living in exile.[1] But a change of location does not necessarily mean a change of heart, and soon the returned exiles found old injustices began to flare up within their social transactions.

We read in Nehemiah 5:1-7 how a group of wealthy, elite Jews exacted usury, or excessively high interest, adding to the plight of the returned exiles. Demanding repayment with such high interest forced the poor to mortgage not only their houses and land, but even to sell their own children into slavery to buy enough grain to survive. Some of their daughters had already been sold to pay their creditors and an anguished cry arose from the people.

---

1. Isaiah 1:5-6

Down through the centuries, such a cry has been echoed by many nations around the world, the anguished cry of "INJUSTICE!" The same cry arose from the earth in accusation of Cain when, out of jealous envy, he spilled Abel's innocent blood. The same cry arose from the Jews who, at the hands of Hitler's henchmen, perished in the hideous holocaust. The same cry arose from the Cambodians who walked through near genocide following two successive waves of massacre by Pol Pot and Viet Cong armies. It is the same cry today of many Afghanis who escaped murder only to be forced to live now as refugees and renegades.

THE CRY OF OUR HEART

Perhaps the same cry is also emerging from the depths of your own heart. As we consider the issue of injustice, we must remember three foundational principles:

1. God is just in all of His ways.
2. Satan is unjust in all of his ways.
3. Man is unjust in many of his ways.

In our world today, much injustice results from man's inhumanity to man. So many are obsessed by an insatiable appetite for position and possessions, corrupted by greed and lust, that people are regarded as usable things and ultimately disposable. Such an obsessive/compulsive disorder has risen to epidemic proportions, resulting in sustained wounding around the world.

"The spirit of a man will sustain his infirmity, but a wounded spirit, who can bear?"[2] What does it mean to be wounded, and how does it affect us? Such painful wounding emanates from the heart or

---

2. Proverbs 18:14, King James Version

spirit of man as a result of the unloving attitudes, actions or words of others. It can be described as a chronic, unrelenting pain arising from a part of man deeper than any organ system. The one who has never felt such a deep heart hurt would be fortunate indeed.

The signs of sustained wounding in the more passive person emerge in the form of self-pity, self-condemnation, morbid introspection, self-hatred, depression and even suicidal tendencies. The more aggressive person, meanwhile, becomes angry, critical, condemning, hateful and even violent to those close to him. These symptoms often reveal a "wounded spirit" that is bearing a person along in the fabric of its pain. Having a wounded spirit may eventually tear at the structure of our lives, impeding significant relationships with others and destroying the nurturing capacity of our own spirit.

If we are unable to bear wounding in our hearts, how are we to deal with it? Is there some other way to handle this thief of life? It has been estimated that we use 50% of our mental and emotional energy alone just to suppress wounds from the past. How can we become free and begin to experience our full measure of life? Can our memories be erased, renewed or reprogrammed?

RECORDINGS OF THE HEART

To better understand our brain's function, let's look at some research by Dr. Wilder Penfield, a neurosurgeon from McGill University in Montreal.[3] In treating patients suffering from focal epilepsy,

---

3. Memory Mechanisms, A.M.A. Achives of Neurology and Psychiatry, 67(1952) pp. 178-198.

Penfield made some exciting observations on memory and emotions during the course of brain surgery. While each patient was under local anesthesia and fully conscious, he stimulated the outer layer, or cortex of the temporal lobe of the brain with a weak electric current.

The responses were remarkable! Past events and their associated emotions surfaced from each patient's subconscious and then "replayed" in detail at the conscious level. Penfield concluded that the events and corresponding emotion were inextricably locked together and stored "on tape" in the temporal cortex of each patient's brain. The electric stimulation not only caused total recall but also a reliving of the events in the mind.

Observations since then have shown that outer stimulations in every day life may have the same effect in surfacing events and related emotions, even as far back as in the womb. When one of these events surface, along with its emotions, how are we to handle it? Is it possible to receive a healing from wounds of the past, lessening the pain? Let us turn to our Creator's life commentary for further insight on these questions.

Speaking through Paul, our Creator instructs us to be "transformed by the renewing of your minds ..." and to be "constantly renewed in the spirit of your mind."[4] But what is "the spirit of our minds" and how can we apply this?

Vincent defined it as "the higher life principle in man by which the human reason, the organ of moral thinking and knowing, is informed."[5] To be changed here is not simply referring to a change in

---

4. Romans 12:2, Ephesians 4:23
5. Marvin Vincent, Word Studies in the New Testament Vol. 3, (Grand Rapids, MI: Eerdmans) p.395.

opinion or doctrine. He says, "'The spirit of the mind' when renewed brings change to both the mind's bent and its materials of thoughts."

RENEWING THE HEART

From these thoughts and scriptures we see that RENEWING is the next reinforcing rod to place in the foundation stone. To heal wounds in the spirit of man, the renewal process is vital.

"This is what the Lord says: 'Your wound is incurable, your injury beyond healing.'" The Lord is speaking here of man's inability to cope with the problem in his own strength. Then the Lord says, "But I will restore you to health and heal your wounds."[6] So, how does God heal our wounds and renew us in the spirit of our minds? What is our responsibility in the process?

Let's look more closely at the word *renew*. One of the Greek verbs translated "to renew" is *"anakainoo."*

In Vine's Expository Dictionary of New Testament Words, the word is divided into two parts: "ana" meaning back or again; and "kainos" meaning new, not recent, but different.[7]

Therefore renewal means to be made new again, to have a new "back" or past. We cannot change *events* of the past, but we can change the reactions and attitudes that emerge from those events, and still affect the spirit of our mind. In addition, this word could easily refer to healing wounds of the past, resulting in new life so, as in Romans 12:2, we can be changed and transformed from the corrosive influences of both the past and

---

6. Jeremiah 30:12,17
7. Vine's Expository Dictionary, op. cit., p.950.

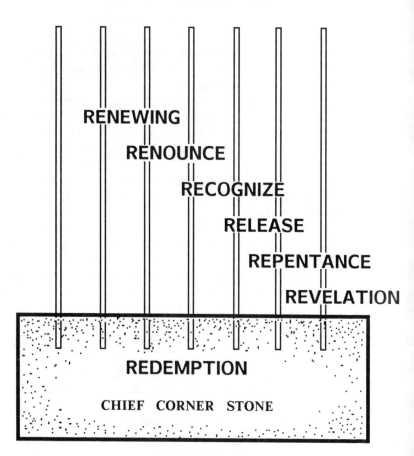

FIGURE 36

present through the renewing of our minds.

HEALING THE HEART

Some people today have questioned whether healing of the heart is a biblical concept. David, reflecting on the return of the exiles and the restoration of Jerusalem, had no doubts:

"He heals the brokenhearted and binds up their wounds - curing their pains and their sorrows."[8] In Revelation we are told of a crystal clear river proceeding from the throne of God with the tree of life on both sides whose very leaves are for "the healing and restoration of the nations."[9]

There can be no doubt that it is God's desire to heal the wounded and brokenhearted. Some say Christians are the only ones who shoot their wounded, and sadly, this is too often true. God has made provision for wounding, just as He has for sin, in the very tree Christ hung upon. As the leaves of the tree of life in Revelation signify restoration, so we are restored by Christ's own tree, the cross, where He was wounded to heal our wounds. The cross is our provision, and Christ's ministry there holds the key to healing the deepest affliction in any Christian.

To understand this mystery, let's consider His redemption described in the Amplified Bible's translation of Isaiah 53:5 and 1 Peter 2:24:

"He was wounded for our transgressions,
He was bruised for our guilt and iniquities
and with the stripes that wounded him we
are healed and made whole."

---

8. Psalm 147:3, Amplified Bible; cf., Psalm 34:18; Isaiah 51:15; Isaiah 61:1; Luke 4:18
9. Revelation 22:2, Amplified Bible

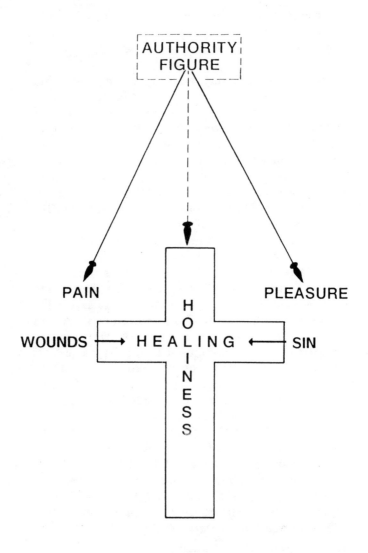

FIGURE 37

"He personally bore our sins in His [own] body to the tree [as to an altar and offered Himself on it], that we might die (cease to exist) to sin and live to righteousness. By His wounds you have been healed."

These verses reveal two important aspects of the ministry of the cross, relating to our previous studies on lust and the pain/pleasure swing. In Figure 37, we see the pain/pleasure swing depicted, swinging from the lustful pleasure relating to sin, over to the inner pain, corresponding with our wounds. The swing back and forth from pain to pleasure can only be stopped on the cross, where we find cleansing from sin and healing for our wounds. These burdens are too heavy for us, and we don't need to bear them. If we attempt to carry them we will be overcome by the shame and pain of our sin, as well as the guilt and bitterness of our wounding. Jesus came that we might have life through His death on the cross. He suffered the injustice, affliction and pain on the cross so that He Himself might bear our injustices in His body, bringing healing to the wounded in spirit.

THE RENEWING PROCESS

Now that we have investigated some of the principles of the renewal process, let's see what happens when we put it into practice. What steps can we take to appropriate healing in our hearts? How do we begin to move toward wholeness and holiness?

ACKNOWLEDGING

Denial of an inner wound is a form of self-manipulation. In the same way, when we suppress hurt, we internalize unhealthy emotional energy which can lead to depression or some other psychosomatic disorder. If we are truly hurting, it is important to accept it and express the truth to yourself. Some believe a Christian should not feel hurt, but this is only a super-spiritual form of suppression with the same consequence as denial. Jesus Himself felt hurt and even wept as he stood before the grave of Lazarus.[10] Later at the Garden of Gethsemane, Jesus' inner pain caused not only tears, but sweat like drops of blood to ooze from His body.[11] It is obvious then, to hurt is not sin, but how we handle it may be.

BELIEVING

Christ bore our pain and grief on the cross. We must also believe He is willing and able to carry our pain and grief today. "For it is by grace you have been saved, through faith - and this not from yourselves, it is the gift of God."[12] Just as we trusted God for salvation from sin, so we must trust Him for healing in a step of faith. As we wrestle with unbelief, we can win by pitting His truth against our sensual input.

Perhaps even now you are asking yourself, "Can God really renew and change me in this area of my life? I've been like this for years!" Yes, He can, and faith gives us the victory!

---

10. John 11:35
11. Luke 22:39-45
12. Ephesians 2:8, New International Version

CONFESSING

We read in Romans 10:9-10 that with our mouth confession is made unto salvation or healing. But we need to confess both our sins and our wounds, accepting responsibility for our own lives. It is so easy to play the blame game for our wounds, blaming parents, teachers, and the guy next door. Of course parents are not perfect. They are also held accountable for their actions, but even while our parents' influence may leave scars in our lives, we also must take responsibility for our sins.

Before making a prayer of confession, we need to look back and review our wounding experiences. Healing is the work and function of the Holy Spirit, so it's important to be led by Him and not just by someone's technique. Take time to linger in prayer over the different stages and phases of your life, allowing the Holy Spirit to supernaturally reveal significant events. Perhaps He will point out some occurrences in the womb, infancy, childhood, adolescence, friendships, or marriage. Often an emotional expression can be an effective entrance point for healing prayer, and a tearful confession becomes more than a catharsis. When mixed with faith, expressing our hurts to God with tears can replace the wounded memories with the healing balm of Jesus' love and understanding. Jesus can and will bear our wounds if we choose to open up the deep places in our hearts to Him.

DESIRING

I've seen over and over that we must truly desire to be healed before our spirits can be healed. Some prefer to be nourished and fed through their wounding, and deep down, do not want to part with it. They may even go through the motions in prayer, but inside, they cannot bear losing their tool for getting attention or "pet" infirmity for fear of being left alone or ignored. Often they drift from counselor to counselor, going over the same ground again and again, until they decide at last nothing works for them. They can't admit that in reality, they are not ready for these keys to work for them. "Blessed are those who hunger and thirst for righteousness for they will be filled."[13] All too often, it is not until we are in a crisis or affliction that we really get thirsty!

EXERCISING

In 1 Timothy 4:7, we read that while physical exercise has some value, we are also to exercise ourselves unto godliness. This is something of far greater value. In the context of renewal or healing, such exercise involves putting off the old reactions and replacing them with new responses.

"Strip yourselves of your former nature - put off and discard your old unrenewed self - which characterized your previous manner of life and becomes corrupt through lusts and desires that spring from delusion; And be constantly renewed in the spirit of your mind - having a fresh mental and spiritual attitude; And put on the new nature [the regenerate self] created in Gods image, [Godlike] in true righteousness and holiness."14

---

13. Matthew 5:6, New International Version
14. Ephesians 4:22-24, Amplified Bible

How can we practically put off the old, and put on the new? In his book *Rational Christian Thinking*, Dr. Gary Sweeten discusses how we arrive at our own personal belief systems, as well as how we can change them.[15]

Sweeten says we first experience an Activating event (A) which then leaves us with a Consequential feeling (C) and results in a Decisive action (D). Based on this chain reaction, we then develop a Belief system (B) around the event, forming the A,B,C,D's of how we develop behavior patterns. Let's use an example to illustrate.

A. ACTIVATING EVENT:
Suppose a black dog leaped out of the shadows, tearing a hole in the seat of a child's pants.

C. CONSEQUENTIAL FEELING:
Fear, anxiety and tension are produced.

D. DECISIVE ACTION:
The child runs away as fast as possible from the dog. Such an experience in childhood can be so traumatic, that years later the adult man or woman may still have the following belief system:

B. BELIEF SYSTEM:
Because this happened, the adult now believes all black dogs are aggressive and dangerous. If a black dog comes into view, all the associated emotions and flight patterns are relived.

---

15. Gary Sweeten, Alice Petersen and Dorothy Geverdt, <u>Rational Christian Thinking</u>, (Cincinnati:Christian Information Committee,1986), p. 67.

For this person to begin to change his emotions and behavior around black dogs, he first must change his belief about them. Only when he is able to accept the truth that many black dogs are kind and gentle, will he retain the healing from his original experience. Then he will begin to feel and act differently around black dogs.

In the same way, we can put off our old, learned behavioral responses and put on the new, if we focus on the truth of God's word, believe it in our hearts, and confess it with our mouths. [See "Come Aside" at the end of the chapter.]

As we look again at 1 Timothy 4:7, notice that *we* are the ones to exercise *ourselves* unto godliness. *We* put off the old and put on the new.

> The truth is to be told.
> Anger is to be controlled.
> The thief is to steal no more.
> The tongue is to be tamed.
> Kindness is to be extended.

To put this into practice, repentance, ongoing confession and honesty must continually accompany renewal, or it won't last in our lives. The Israelites longed for God to heal their wounds, but God responded that He did not really know what to do with them![16] Instead He compares their repentance to a cloud or morning dew that disappears faster than it appears. How can God heal them on that basis? One of God's greatest challenges is not our desire for His gifts of grace, but our refusal to grow into His likeness. Unless healing is accompanied by putting off old and putting on new responses, it can only be temporary. Only as we

---

16. Hosea 6:1-4

exercise ourselves unto godliness can we maintain growth and establish genuine healing.

FORGIVING

We are to forgive one another readily, freely and abundantly, as God in Christ forgave us,[17] but all too often we fall into the snare of bitterness and resentment toward others. The most classic illustration is the story of the unforgiving servant in Matthew 18:23-35 who, after being forgiven his debt by his master, turned around and refused to forgive a much smaller debt, putting the man in jail.

What many of us fail to see is that the servant never truly received his master's unconditional forgiveness. All he received was what he asked for, an extension of time to pay back the "$10 million" debt. Because he hadn't received forgiveness in his heart, he also could not give it - the unforgiven became unforgiving and the unaccepted became unaccepting. Therefore, he could not even forgive a mere "$20" debt and put the debtor in jail.

Many confess they are forgiven, but have not received the forgiveness in their hearts to impart freedom to their lives. Instead they become grievance collectors, treasuring each irritation, slight or injury. They pigeonhole for safekeeping a record of each wrong, endorsing every injustice with their debtor's name on the back. Locked in a web of hurt, they hurt others; feeling unforgiven, they struggle to forgive others; considering themselves as failures, they fail others; believing they are rejected, they reject others, and so on. The act of "forgiving ourselves" only has value after we ob-

---

17. Ephesians 4:32

tain God's forgiveness. If we have not received
God's forgiveness *in our hearts*, we cannot forgive
from our hearts, others or ourselves. We must take
our guilt and shame to God and obtain His pardon.
When we don't, we are like the tragic young man
who was released from a lifetime prison sentence,
but yet through unbelief was unable to walk to
freedom through the open prison doors. To be
healed, we must learn to freely forgive ourselves
from the heart.

GROWING

The challenge Paul gives us is to graduate from
drinking milk to digesting the meat of real spiritual
food.[18] "Grow up!" he says, calling us to grow up
into Christ by speaking the truth in love to one another. Some freely speak out truth that devastates,
while others try to love in silence by keeping the
peace. If growth in godliness is to occur, we need
both in balance. Old wounds still festering can
leave ugly scars in our personality and halt our
spiritual and character growth.

HELPING

As we have received, so we should give. God
promises healing to spring forth speedily if we
work to set the captives free, feed the hungry,
house the homeless, clothe the naked and give ourselves to loving sacrifice.[19] In Africa, a surgeon
faced a dilemma when the relatives of a patient all
wanted to daily file by and inspect his surgical
wound. Finally, to prevent infection and allow the

---

18. Hebrews 5:11-14
19. Isaiah 58:8

wound to heal, the surgeon made a dressing with a window in it. Some of us are like those relatives, continually inspecting the wounds of our hearts through introspection. Once our Great Physician has brought us through a time of spiritual surgery, let's leave our recovery to Him. As we care for the needs of the poor and downtrodden, the Lord promises to mend us: "... *then your light will rise in the darkness, and your night will become like the noonday. The Lord will guide you always; He will satisfy your needs in a sun-scorched land and will strengthen your frame. You will be like a well-watered garden, like a spring whose waters never fail.*"[20]

All of the steps we have now reviewed are very important to the renewal process. Only as we give ourselves diligently to apply them to our lives will our healing spring forth! Now we have sunk six iron reinforcing rods into the foundation stone, enabling us to firmly build the walls of salvation. In the last chapter, we will drive the final rod into the stone and go on to see the walls of personality completed with the walls of salvation and the gates of praise.

COME ASIDE

Reflect on significant trauma-activating events in your life.

What undesirable emotional and behavioral patterns have remained with you since each event?

What false belief system did you accept as a result

---

20. Isaiah 58:10-11, New International Version

of that event?

If you recognize a need and a desire for change:
1. Allow the Lord to bring healing to the memory of the event.
2. Tell God you reject your old beliefs, and then accept and begin to confess your new and true beliefs out loud to God, and yourself several times a day. (Romans 10:9-10)

CHAPTER 15

A DIFFERENT CHARACTER EMERGES

The last reinforcing rod to be placed in the foundation stone will enable us to cement the rest of the blocks together to form the wall of salvation. This iron rod of REBUILDING assumes the wall will continue to be built, in light of the truth that salvation is a process of becoming more and more immersed in Jesus. Our goal is expressed for us by Paul in his letter to the Galatians: "It is no longer I who live but Christ who lives in me."[1]

We read in Nehemiah 2:18, "I also told them about the gracious hand of my God upon me and what the King had said to me. They replied, 'Let us start *rebuilding*.' So they began this good work." So Nehemiah and his co-workers began rebuilding and when they were almost done, we read how there were no gaps left.[2] All that was left to do was put the gates in the gateways.

---

1. Galatians 2:20, Revised Standard Version
2. Nehemiah 6:1

THE WALL OF SALVATION

NEHEMIAH = RESTORATION
EZRA = RECONCILIATION

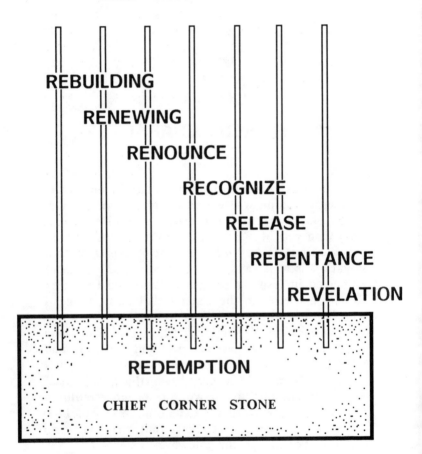

REBUILDING
RENEWING
RENOUNCE
RECOGNIZE
RELEASE
REPENTANCE
REVELATION

REDEMPTION

CHIEF CORNER STONE

FIGURE 38

Before we delve further into the symbolism surrounding the completed walls of Jerusalem, let's look at what those gates represent and their significance for us today while we set them in place in the wall of salvation. The gates of Jerusalem were the entrance and exit points of the city, bringing in and letting out all that is vital to the upkeep and health of the inhabitants. Often guards kept watch of the traffic, ensuring that what came in and out of the gates was acceptable to the city magistrates. As we look at the characteristics of city gates, let's consider them as the doorways to our own lives.

GUARDING THE GATES

When gates are broken down, undefended or unguarded, an enemy can easily gain entrance, ransack, plunder and destroy a city. Many lives have been ransacked and even destroyed because they left their eye- or ear-gates unguarded. At the same time, gates that are rusted, closed up, or kept under lock and key may not permit the disposal of city garbage and set the stage for rampant disease and even death. The crisis may be compounded if adequate food and water supplies are not carried through the gates. We must carefully watch the gates in our lives, for what comes through may easily capture and even corrupt our hearts. We are told, "Keep and guard your heart with all vigilance and above all that you guard, for out of it flow the springs of life."[3] Because *gates* are the entrances to our hearts, we must guard them in order to keep our hearts.

---

3. Proverbs 4:23, Amplified Bible

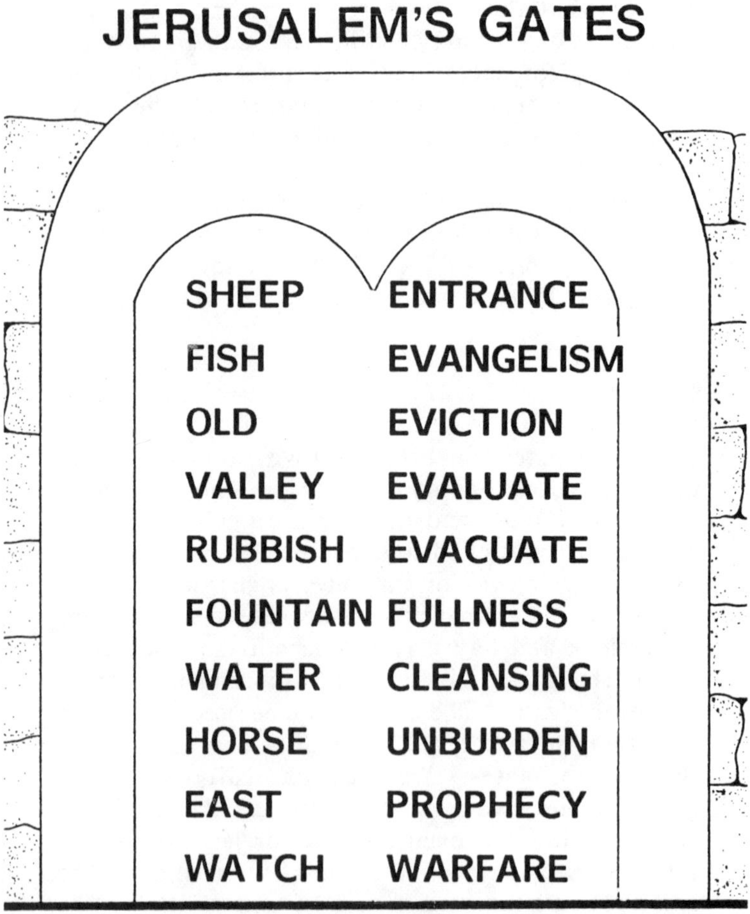

JERUSALEM'S GATES

SHEEP	ENTRANCE
FISH	EVANGELISM
OLD	EVICTION
VALLEY	EVALUATE
RUBBISH	EVACUATE
FOUNTAIN	FULLNESS
WATER	CLEANSING
HORSE	UNBURDEN
EAST	PROPHECY
WATCH	WARFARE

FIGURE 39

We see in Figure 39 the list of gates around the walls of Jerusalem, taken from Nehemiah 3. This is not only a list of the gates, but also of those volunteering to build, and the nobles who felt that the work was beneath their dignity. As we look at each gate, we will examine the significance of its name and examine its application for our lives today.

SHEEP GATE ----- ENTRANCE

"Therefore Jesus said again, 'I tell you the truth, I am the gate for the sheep. ...whoever enters through Me will be saved. He will come in and go out and find pasture.'"[4] As we read on in John 10, we see how Jesus contrasts His role as the Good Shepherd with that of the thieves and robbers who try to destroy the sheep. Jesus says theives will not enter through His gate of salvation, but will skirt the wall in secret, attempting to steal lives and inheritances from the unwary and unprotected.

In the same way, we must enter life through the sheep gate, or we will not begin to partake of our inheritance. Through the finished work of redemption by Jesus on the cross, we can go in and out of the gate to have fellowship with the Father. Jesus needs to have this place in our hearts, reigning as Lord and Savior. The sheep gate speaks of ENTRANCE into the inheritance of our lives.

FISH GATE ----- EVANGELISM

When Jesus first met Andrew, Peter, James and John, they were casting their fishing nets by the

---

4. John 10:7-9, New International Version

sea of Galilee. He told them to come follow Him, and He would make them fishers of men.[5] They immediately left their nets, and followed Him.

Today Jesus makes the same call to us, with the same promise of making us fishers of men. The fish gate speaks of the great commission given in Matthew 28:18-20 to go into all the world and preach the gospel to every tribe and nation. With every opportunity, we should reach out and share the good news of Jesus Christ. God says, "... he who wins souls is wise."[6] Let's never forget the priceless value of a lost soul. Even the newest Christian can introduce another to his newly found Friend and Savior.

At Pacific and Asia Christian University (PACU), where I serve as the dean of the College of Counseling and Health Care, our major mandate is to reach this generation with the gospel of Jesus Christ. Training programs and degree courses are all built around this central theme, and from health care to theology, the goal is to reach the lost. We are learning to meet felt needs, progressively touching the deeper eternal needs in the heart of man in our education for evangelism.

OLD GATE ----- EVICTION

The old gate speaks of our "old self" with its anger, curses, slander and lying, and evil practices. That old, unregenerate self must be EVICTED, put away, got rid of![7] In its place we are to clothe ourselves with the new self, being renewed after the likeness of Him who created it. "... put on the

---

5. Matthew 4:18-22
6. Proverbs 11:30, New International Version
7. Colossians 3:8-9, Amplified Bible

new self, which is being renewed in knowledge in the image of its Creator."[8]

But this putting off the old self is where renewal is often hindered. Unless we embrace this process wholeheartedly, we won't genuinely grow. The following equations illustrate this truth.

Put off - Put on = No change
Put on - Put off = Shortchange
Put off + Put on = Real change

All too many of us shortchange ourselves and unnecessarily struggle for years. True change can come, but it won't last until the old self has been put to death with Christ on the cross, destroying the power of the sinful self to make us slaves to sin.[9] Even as Jesus did, most of us cringe from the cross. But He made it clear that unless we crucify our flesh daily we cannot be His disciple. If we try to be a Christian without embracing the cross to *evict* the old unregenerate self, we will stumble and fall.

VALLEY GATE ----- EVALUATE

"Even though I walk through the VALLEY of the shadow of death, I will fear no evil, for you are with me...."[10] All of us walk through valleys in our lives, places of testing and trial. Here is where we learn about our own hearts.

In 1980, during the height of the Vietnam/ Cambodian exodus, I was working in a refugee hospital in Thailand on the border of Cambodia.

---

8. Colossians 3:10, New International Version
9. Romans 6:6
10. Psalm 23:4, New International Version

One morning, while making rounds in the medical ward, I watched as two American physicians came in, tired and disheveled. They told me they had been sent to relieve another physician in a small bush hospital in Cambodia, but had been held at gunpoint and could not sleep through the nights of constant gunfire. At last they decided discretion was the better part of valor, and after only a day or two in Cambodia, they gave up and crossed the border back into Thailand.

As I listened sympathetically, I heard a still small voice prompting me to offer to replace them. Knowing it was the voice of God, I obeyed and told them I would go. Almost immediately, I began to go through my own valley of the shadow of death. Facing the possibility of being killed by the Viet Cong or becoming a prisoner of war, I knew I might never see my wife and boys again.

As this realization hit me, I began to weep as a deep battle raged within. Who did I love most - God or my family? Did I truly love God with all my heart? Could I trust Him? Was He with me? The test was in my obedience, and I knew it.

Going back to the tiny, crowded room that served as my bedroom, I began to write a note to my family: "My dearest, precious ones ..." Suddenly I began to weep uncontrollably, and tears splashed onto the page as thoughts of never seeing them again swept over me. In my head I knew I should obey God and go, but my heart and emotions protested in anguish.

Maybe I wasn't supposed to go after all. Maybe I should stay where I was! But I finally finished the tear-stained note and as I gave instructions to a friend about delivering the letter, I again began to weep. Gripped afresh with the possible outcome of my obedience, I counted the cost and chose to obey and relieve the doctor at the hospital in Cambodia. As it turned out, God went with me and, although the bush hospital was bombed after I left, God brought me safely back to my family in Hawaii.

I learned first hand that times of testing strengthen our resolve and purify our hearts and motives, while those valleys of weeping become a pilgrimage to Zion. "Passing through the VALLEY of weeping they make it a place of springs; ... They go from strength to strength ..."[11]

RUBBISH GATE ----- EVACUATE

"But whatever was to my profit, I now consider loss for the sake of Christ. What is more, I consider everything a loss compared to the surpassing greatness of knowing Christ Jesus my Lord, for whose sake I have lost all things. I consider them RUBBISH, that I may gain Christ ..."[12]

It is evident that Paul was no garbage collector! Anything not expedient was evacuated and thrown from his life. Some of us gather so much garbage along life's way we become immobilized by it. Bound by our belongings, we forget we first belong to Christ. Paul laid aside every weight, including sin, so nothing could hamper him from winning the prize of life itself. Whenever we stumble over our garbage, let's rush it to the rubbish gate and leave it there for good.

YWAM health care teams in the Philippines minister at the huge rubbish dump of greater Manila, where every day, several thousand village squatters sift and sort through garbage mounds with little picks, searching for anything at all to recycle.

---

11. Psalm 84:6-7, Amplified Bible
12. Philippians 3:7-8, New International Version

How many of us are also rubbish recyclers, trying to sort through the rubbish of our lives in hopes of using it again? Instead, we need to EVACUATE it out of our lives once and for all.

FOUNTAIN GATE ----- FULLNESS

"If anyone is thirsty, let him come to me and drink. Whoever believes in Me, as the Scripture has said, streams of living water will flow from within him."[13]

Jesus is speaking of the Holy Spirit, who will flow from within us as streams of living water when we allow Him entrance at the Fountain Gate. Jesus knew that without the FULLNESS of the Holy Spirit the disciples would have no power to witness or do His works, so He asked them to wait in Jerusalem for the promised fullness.[14] The story of the actions of the Holy Spirit working through those who were available to Him is told throughout the book of Acts. We are further commanded to continue "being filled" with the Holy Spirit, not imbibing the wines of worldliness.[15] If we bypass the fountain gate, we can only serve God in our own strength and power, inadequate for the many challenges of a life of service for Him. "... 'Not by might nor by power, but by my Spirit,' says the Lord Almighty."[16]

WATER GATE ----- CLEANSING

"Husbands love your wives, as Christ loved the

---

13. John 7:37-38, New International Version
14. Acts 1:4
15. Ephesians 5:18
16. Zechariah 4:6, New International Version

church and gave Himself up for her, so that He might sanctify her, having cleansed her by the washing of water with the Word, that He might present the church to Himself in glorious splendor, without spot or wrinkle or any such things - that she might be holy and faultless."[17]

The Word of God is like water to cleanse us. We need to bathe ourselves in the truth of God's Word daily, memorizing and meditating on it. As we do so, our hearts are kept clean from the daily stains of sin.

Once on vacation from medical school, I had a job laying drains with a gang of "street wise" men. It didn't take long for me to realize their mouths were as foul as the sewage we were laying drains for. After a few days I found myself beginning to think in their language, and I cried out to God in concern. Soon He led me into intensive memorization of scripture, and whenever a foul word came into my mind, I quoted scripture in its place. I found the Word is so powerful, it not only kept my mind and heart clean throughout the work day but was like a sharp sword, driving off attacks of the enemy.

HORSE GATE ----- UNBURDEN

"Come to me, all you who labor and are heavy-laden and overburdened, and I will cause you to rest [I will ease and relieve and refresh your souls.]"[18]

Horses are great burden bearers, enabling man to achieve in all kinds of circumstances down through the centuries. So we see the Horse Gate is

---

17. Ephesians 5:25-27, Amplified Bible
18. Matthew 11:28

where we unload burdens of anxiety, sin, guilt, resentment, hurt and much more into the hands of Jesus. As we read on in Matthew 11, He promises to exchange our heavy load for His light yoke, but still so many of us go on carrying our weighted burdens. He longs to take them from us, and give us the light yoke of learning to obey and trust Him with all of our concerns. We are also told not to be anxious about anything, but in everything entrust ourselves into His hands by prayer.[19] All too often we forget this and begin to worry, only praying in a crisis. "Look at the birds of the air; they do not sow or reap or store away in barns, and yet your heavenly Father feeds them. Are you not much more valuable than they? Who of you by worrying can add a single hour to his life?"[20]

The more burdens we choose to carry, the less of life we live. But there remains a rest for each one of us: "Therefore while the promise of entering His rest still holds and is offered [today], let us be afraid [to distrust it] ... For we who have believed ... do enter into that rest ..."[21]

EAST GATE ----- PROPHECY

Much of the prophecy in the Bible speaks of the Middle East, and we need to be knowledgeable intercessors for Israel. The reliability of biblical prophecy is confirmed by former events of history surrounding Jesus as well as the Jews. We need to study to understand future prophecies fully and to pray through God's plans for the closure of this age and the ushering in of the next. "Your Kingdom

---

19. Philippians 4:6
20. Matthew 6:26-27, New International Version
21. Hebrews 4:1-3, Amplified Bible

come, Your will be done, on earth as it is in heaven."[22]

WATCH GATE ----- WARFARE.

"I have set watchmen upon your walls, O Jerusalem, who will never hold their peace day or night; you who [are His servants and by your prayers] put the Lord in remembrance [of His promises], keep not silence, and give Him no rest until He establishes Jerusalem and makes it a praise in the earth."[23]

In these verses lie the greatest challenge for the church today. Unless through prayer we engage ourselves in battle in the heavenlies, we do not stand a chance in overcoming all Satan has arrayed against the church. God has equipped us with weapons that are not carnal but mighty to pull down the enemy's strongholds,[24] but, if we don't use them - we will lose the battle.

One of the most pressing needs in the church today is for intercessors who give the Lord no rest until He answers. We in Youth With A Mission saw we could only begin to fulfill God's call as a mission when we began incorporating intercession into our lifestyle. In the same way, the church will only experience renewal when a band of "watchmen" or "watchwomen" are willing to war in the heavenlies through fasting, faith and prayer. In addition, we as individuals will see the fulfillment of God's promises in our lives only when we personally engage ourselves in regular prayer and spiritual warfare. Watch, pray and stand fast!

---

22. Matthew 6:10
23. Isaiah 62:6-7, Amplified Bible
24. 1 Corinthians 10:3-5

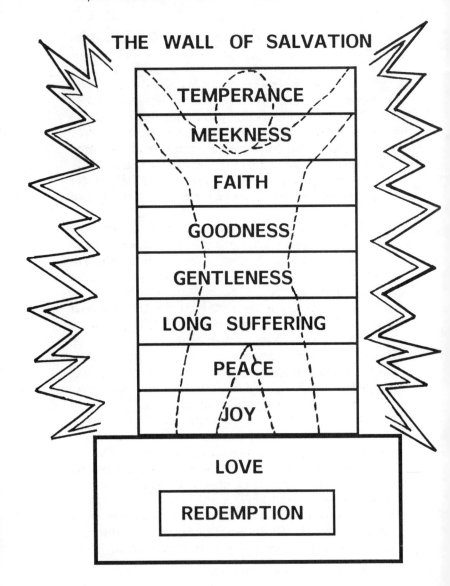

FIGURE 40

As we look again at the SHEEP GATE, we see that when the other gates are in place and functioning in the wall of salvation, we can enter by the sheep gate into a rich and blessed relationship with Jesus. "When he has brought his own sheep outside, he walks on before them, and the sheep follow him, because they know his voice."[25]

When we know Jesus goes before us and recognize His voice from among many, we are in the most exciting and fulfilling place to live. If we are willing and obedient, we can all have this joy and privilege.

Looking in Psalm 24, we read of another reference to *gates*, where David tells us only those with clean hands and pure hearts will enter into His temple. Telling us to seek His face and keep on seeking Him, that we may stand before Him, David then bursts into the central refrain: "Lift up your heads, O you gates; and be lifted up, you age-abiding doors; that the King of glory may come in. Who is the King of glory? ..."[26]

We need to place our gates in position, in the walls, ushering the way for the King of Glory to enter as David's question resounds:

"WHO IS THIS KING OF GLORY?"

The answer is found when we place block on block to complete the WALL OF SALVATION.

"For GOD so *loved* the world that he gave his one and only Son, that whoever believes in him shall not perish but have eternal life."[27]

This word reveals the truth of who our King of Glory is. In God's great plan of redemption, it is evident that love is the cornerstone upon which

---

25. John 10:4, Amplified Bible
26. Psalm 24:7-8, Amplified Bible
27. John 3:16, New International Version

all the walls are built, because God is love. Christ paid the supreme sacrifice so we would not perish. Until we experience that love, we cannot complete the wall of salvation.

"O Israel, hope in the Lord! For with the Lord there is mercy and loving-kindness, and with Him is plenteous redemption."[28]

The King of Glory is:

> LOVE
> JOY
> PEACE
> LONG SUFFERING
> GENTLENESS
> GOODNESS
> FAITH
> MEEKNESS
> TEMPERANCE.

The only one who fits this description is the King of Glory! When that King of Glory becomes both resident and president in our lives, His likeness begins to emerge in us. It is then the wall of salvation begins to take shape in the completeness of our personality:

"... that [we might arrive] at really mature manhood (the completeness of personality which is nothing less than the standard height of Christ's own perfection), the measure of the stature of the fulness of the Christ and the completeness found in Him."[29]

CONCLUSION

As we have gone through the process of rebuilding the walls of our hearts in line with the

---

28. Psalm 130:7, Amplified Bible
29. Ephesians 4:13, Amplified Bible

Divine Plumbline, I trust God has opened your life in a new way. We have seen how the enemy often deceives us into building unstable walls of rejection and rebellion by following false human plumblines in our lives. Pride and unbelief must be repented of and dealt with before these walls can be torn down and replaced with new sturdy walls in our hearts, walls in line with God's plumbline. These walls of salvation reflect the true image and nature of God, and as we continue to embrace and live by His Plumbline, we become sons and daughters of God.

When the walls of our heart are continually built in line with the Divine Plumbline, we will find the well of our heart to be full and overflowing with salvation. Soon others will come to our wells and drink from that well of living water as we experience a personal wholeness and holiness we have never known before.

We read that the eyes of the Lord move to and fro throughout the earth, searching for the one whose heart is perfect toward Him, or whose heart is in line with His Divine Plumbline.[30] Let us resolve to be among those who allow God to rebuild our lives. Then we will find ourselves not only strengthened and blessed, receiving our full inheritance, but also used by God to show forth the glory of His image and fulfill His purposes on the earth. We will then find our lives are just like the city described by the prophet Isaiah, not only strong, but sparkling with His glory:

"O afflicted city, lashed by storms and not comforted. I will build you with stones of turquoise, your foundations with sapphires. I will

---

30. 2 Chronicles 16:9

make your battlements of rubies, your gates of sparkling jewels, and all your walls of precious stones."[31]

---

31. Isaiah 54:11-12, New International Version

BIBLIOGRAPHY AND RESOURCES

Thomas Verney and John Kelly, *The Secret Life of the Unborn Child*, (New York:Summit Books,1987).

The Amplified Bible, (Grand Rapids:Zondervan, 1965).

Gary Sweeten, Alice Peterson, Dorothy Geverdt, *Rational Christian Thinking*, (Cincinatti:Christian Information Committee, 1987).

William Backus and Marie Chapian, *Telling Yourself The Truth*, (Minneapolis:Bethany House Publishers, 1980).

Floyd McClung, *The Father Heart of God*, (Eugene, OR:Harvest House Publishers, 1985).

Charles R. Solomon, *The Rejection Syndrome*, (Wheaton, IL:Tyndale House, 1982).

David A. Seamonds, *Healing for Damaged Emotions*, (Wheaton, IL:Victor Books [a division of S.P. Publications], 1981).

Lawrence J. Crabb, Jr., *Effective Biblical Counseling*, (Grand Rapids:Zondervan, 1977).

Gary R. Collins, *Christian Counseling*, (Waco, TX:Word Books, 1980).

Everett L. Shostrom, *Man, The Manipulator*, (Nashville:Abingdon Press, 1967).

Tom Marshall, *Free Indeed*, (Auckland, New Zeland:Orama Christian Fellowship Trust, 1975, 5 volumes; 1984, 1 volume revision).

Leanne Payne, *Broken Image*, (Westchester, IL:Crossway Books, 1981).

William Backus, *Telling the Truth to Troubled People*, (Minneapolis:Bethany House Publishers, 1985).

WORDS OF ENDORSEMENT

Dr. Thompson does an excellent job of showing the history and results of our building walls of protection about ourselves. He also makes it abundantly clear that freedom does not come by our tearing down one stone at a time, but rather, we must be set free from bondage to the flesh (our real prison) by the Holy Spirit's making the Cross (Galatians 2:20) a reality in our lives as believers.

Charles R. Solomon, Ed. D.
President and Founder,
Grace Fellowship International

Dr. Thompson takes his readers on a journey into wholeness. Likening the psychological defenses to self-constructed walls raised under the influence of various agencies described as false prophets, this writer measures these walls against the divine plumbline of God's Law, shows the reader how to change through repentance, and describes the renewed life. Careful attention is paid to the problem of misbeliefs in the self-talk, how they originate, and how they can be replaced by the truth of God's Word. Dr. Thompson has supplied graphic line drawings to aid understanding with Scriptural imagery.

William Backus, Ph. D.
Author of "Telling Yourself The Truth",
Founder and Director,
Center For Christian Psychological Services,
St. Paul, Minnesota

With a physician's sure touch in *Walls Of My Heart*, Dr. Thompson dissects the deepest problems of human personality. But this serves as a merciful prelude to healing and reconstruction.

Derek Prince, International Bible Teacher
Jerusalem, Israel

"Dr. Bruce" as we affectionately call him, ministers life out of a great heart of love. Whether by his speaking ministry or written word, you will find he reaches into your soul, diagnoses the problem, and prescribes the "right medicine" for your need. He has ministered on every continent, to people of varying societies and, through this book, he will minister to you.

Loren Cunningham
President
Youth With A Mission International

Having had the privilege of observing the development of Dr. Bruce and Barbara Thompson's lives and ministry for many years, it is with pleasure I endorse this new publication, *Walls Of My Heart*. As one who has travelled extensively throughout the world, I have encountered many people of diverse cultures whose lives have been transformed by their ministry, and others who have been better equipped as counselors by using these practical and biblically-based principles.

Ken Wright
Pastor-Teacher
New Zealand

Bruce Thompson has special insight into the things that hold us back from receiving the full love of the Father. His teaching contains powerful truths that have impacted my life, and the lives of many around me. I am deeply grateful for his sensitivity to the Lord, and his willingness to share this life-changing message with others through his book, *Walls Of My Heart*.

Melody Green
President
Last Days Ministries

Write for your **FREE CATALOG** from:

CROWN MINISTRIES
INTERNATIONAL

SPIRITUAL WARFARE by Dean Sherman
This series is a study for every growing Christian. Dean explores the many dynamics and strategies of *spiritual warfare;* "... for our struggle is not against flesh and blood, but against ... the spiritual forces of wickedness in heavenly places." This series consists of ten, forty-minute sessions available on video cassettes or audio tapes. The accompanying 80-page, illustrated workbook is key to bringing the teaching into visual focus and application.

Video Series - $150.00   Audio Album - $24.95   Workbook - $5.50

ACTS ALIVE! by David Buehring
Acts Alive! is a comprehensive discipleship training program that provides a framework for character formation and follow-through in daily Christian living. The video and audio tapes are available in nine, forty-minute sessions. The 148-page study guide is an exhaustive outline of all the materials discussed. It will challenge and equip each Christian who works to apply the principles revealed.

Video Series - $99.00   Audio Album - $24.95   Study Guide - $7.95

RELATIONSHIPS by Dean Sherman
What is the number one problem in the world? POOR RELATIONSHIPS! In this series Dean effectively challenges each human being to become an answer to the world's greatest problem. No matter what your age or experience, if you have been damaged in the area of relationships, you will be ministered to and blessed by this teaching. There are seven, sixty-minute sessions in the video and audio series. The 80-page illustrated workbook is a needed tool.

Video Series - $150.00   Audio Album - $24.95   Workbook - $5.50

Dynamic, new dimensions in video teaching for your Church, home fellowship or discipleship training school:

KINGDOM SESSION VIDEO SERIES

KINGDOM SESSION I

A basic discipleship course for those who want to strengthen their biblical foundations, including:

The Character of God
The Lordship of Christ
Divine Guidance
Developing a Prayer Life
Authority of Scripture
. . . and others.

KINGDOM SESSION II

A course designed to introduce and implement powerful biblical principles of witnessing and personal evangelism:

Friendship Evangelism
Making Disciples
Dynamics of Personal Witnessing
Understanding the Western Mind
. . . and others.

KINGDOM SESSION III

An insightful presentation of missiology and current mission trends, as well as a valuable training in:

Cross-cultural Witnessing
Trans-line Local Church Linking
Cultural Orientation for Specific Nations
. . . and much more.

Crown Ministries International has video teaching which incorporates these and other exciting materials for building maturity in the Body of Christ. Teachers include: Steve Fry, Dick Eastman, Floyd McClung, Winkie Pratney, Rick Olson, Winkie Pratney, John Dawson, Jack Hayford and others.

Available from Crown Ministries International:

The Divine Plumbline
by Dr. Bruce Thompson

The material presented in this book is available to you on
video cassettes or audio tapes to be used with an accompanying study guide. These tools have been used all
across the world with much encouraging feedback. Whether
used in a small home study or a larger church setting, these
principles have been used to lead many people to new
dimensions of freedom and usefulness in the Kingdom of
God. The series has come from years of counseling both in
medical practice and on the mission field.

Video Series	15/40 min. sessions	$275.00
Audio Album	15/40 min. tapes	49.95
Study Guide	128 pages (illustrated)	7.95

*Dr. Bruce Thompson's series shows how God's plumbline exposes the
false teachings of humanism and the evil results of building our lives on rejection, rebellion, unbelief and pride. We highly recommend this ministry,
geared to help people in a very practical and spiritual way.*

Harold J. Brokke, Principal
Bethany Missionary Fellowship

*I wholeheartedly endorse the powerful and effective ministry God has
given my friend, Dr. Bruce Thompson. The man lives his message; therefore, he speaks with authority.*

Joy Dawson
International Bible Teacher

You may order any of the videos, audios, study guides or receive a free
catalog by writing **Crown Ministries International, P.O. Box 49, Euclid,
MN, 56722 - Phone (218) 745-5826.** When ordering a video, indicate
VHS or BETA format. Payment must accompany orders payable in U.S.
funds. Checks and money orders accepted. Enclose 3% additional for
shipping and handling of video orders, 10% addditional for study guides
and audio albums. Shipping and handling charges for foreign orders will
be billed if they exceed charges listed above. Please allow 2-4 weeks for
delivery. Time may be longer on foreign orders.